THE SECRET LIFE OF MOVIES

SIMON BREW

THE SECRET LIFE OF MOVIES

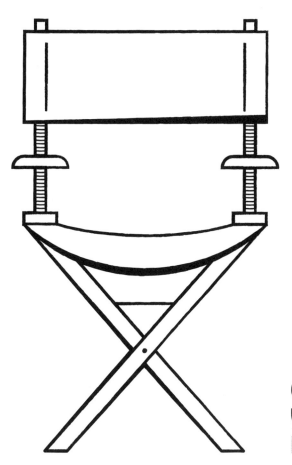

HIDDEN HINTS,
MOTIFS, REFERENCES
AND BACKGROUND
DETAIL IN THE
GREATEST MOVIES

FROM THE FOUNDER OF
DEN OF GEEK

SIMON BREW

FOREWORD BY KIM NEWMAN

An Hachette UK Company
www.hachette.co.uk

First published in Great Britain in 2019
by Cassell, an imprint of
Octopus Publishing Group Ltd
Carmelite House
50 Victoria Embankment
London EC4Y 0DZ
www.octopusbooks.co.uk

Design and Layout Copyright © Octopus Publishing Group 2019
Text Copyright © Simon Brew 2019

Distributed in the US by
Hachette Book Group
1290 Avenue of the Americas
4th and 5th Floors
New York, NY 10104

Distributed in Canada by
Canadian Manda Group
664 Annette St.
Toronto, Ontario, Canada M6S 2C8

ISBN 978-1-78840-127-2

A CIP catalogue record for this book is available from the British Library.

Printed and bound in China

10 9 8 7 6 5 4 3 2 1

Publishing Director: Trevor Davies
Senior Editor: Pollyanna Poulter
Copy Editor: Sonya Newland
Designer: Jack Storey
Picture Research: Giulia Hetherington, Jennifer Veall and Nick Wheldon
Production Controller: Grace O'Byrne

Design and illustration by James Round. See more at www.jamesrounddesign.com

CONTENTS

FOREWORD   6

Clues, Hat Tips and Hidden Details   8

Working Around Production Challenges   32

Details, Choices and Moments   56

On-Set Moments   82

Inspirations and Ramifications   108

Homages, Motifs and Cross-References   130

Sets and Locations   152

Fixed It in Post-Production   174

Cameos, Appearances and Crossovers   194

A Few Last Things...   214

REFERENCES   232
PICTURE CREDITS   235
INDEX   236
ACKNOWLEDGEMENTS   240

FOREWORD

The story goes – and it's been repeated so many times, including as the titles of several books, that it no longer matters whether it actually happened or has been embroidered by world-class tale-spinners – that star Ingrid Bergman came to director Alfred Hitchcock after a sleepless night of worry over the motivation of the character she was playing. The English auteur dismissed her concerns by declaring that "it's only a movie, Ingrid."

That statement resounds – several horror films emblazon their posters with the tagline "keep telling yourself – it's only a movie". Everyone who's ever given more than a minute's thought to making or writing about films has put up with some breezier soul telling them not to be so fussed about such a trivial, passing form. It used to be a convention that filmgoers didn't check the film start times before buying tickets and would go into the auditorium while a film was well underway, sit through it till the end, watch a second feature – plus newsreels, ads and a cartoon – then catch up with the beginning of the film they'd seen the end of and leave the cinema "where we came in".

The man who did the most to put a stop to that approach was Alfred Hitchcock (him again), who insisted patrons not be admitted while *Psycho* (1960) was running. He reasoned that he'd worked hard to deliver what was then a stunning twist ending, so it was only fair that audiences pay attention. Hitch happily told stars "it's only a movie", but he felt there was no "only" about his own films. Self-deprecating in a way only a true genius egoist can be, he deliberately worked in a field (romantic suspense) that few critics who weren't French took seriously. There's little that is haphazard or accidental about his meticulously storyboarded, pre-planned and worked-out-to-the-last-detail films. Even his in-jokes – like his celebrated personal appearances, such as the before-and-after of a weight reduction ad in a newspaper glimpsed in *Lifeboat* (1944) – are supremely crafted.

Anyone who's ever suggested any given film might be saying something has heard the phrase "you're reading too much into it". I remember the film critic Tom Tunney talking about a crucial scene in John Ford's *The Man Who Shot Liberty Valance* (1963) when John Wayne leaves a political meeting and is framed against a pair of posters which highlight the moral quandary his character is in. Someone in the room pooh-poohed Tom's interpretation by saying the posters just happened to be there, and were in the back of frame just because it was more interesting than a bare backdrop. Tom pointed out the fact – obvious, but surprisingly easy to overlook – that Ford didn't shoot the film on location in 1873. Those posters were there because the art department put them there – after someone did research to find authentic posters of the period or worked up convincing fakes. The text on the posters might or might not have been specified in the script, but didn't just appear by magic. If John Ford didn't want them there, he'd have damn well torn them down himself.

Even filmmakers like John Cassavetes or Robert Altman, more disposed to improvisation and "happy accident" than Hitchcock and Ford, micro-manage what's on the screen when they edit their footage. Altman miked up all his actors and had them improvise through long takes with the camera at a discreet distance – one shot in *Buffalo Bill and the Indians* (1976) was taken by a camera *several miles* away from the actors – but when it came to scissors and tape he crafted his films the way a collagist puts together a picture. A DVD issue of *Gosford Park* (2001) includes unused scenes that *haven't* been sound-edited, which gives an insight into just how much craft and consideration Altman put into selecting the bits of mumbled throwaway he wanted heard and ensuring they were audible while less significant chatter faded into the soundscape.

Even unplanned stuff – like the frisky horse which seems to nudge Keith Carradine into proposing to Cristina Raines in Ridley Scott's *The Duellists* (1977) – has to survive the edit, and Scott must have rejected takes in which the nag was better (or worse) behaved to get this perfect moment into the finished film. Audiences accept as a given that movies are like dreams – some of the most powerful seem to channel unconscious fantasies – and, as such, are magic. But people make them. People think about them

before and after they're on a screen. What you see and hear is what you get, but then it's up to you to look closer, like Bruce Willis pondering his relationship to Hitchcock's *Vertigo* (1958) in Terry Gilliam's *Twelve Monkeys* (1996)..."the movie never changes. It *can't* change. But every time you see it, it seems different, because you're different." In this book, you'll learn a lot about films – but, going back and watching them again with this book in mind, you might also learn a lot about yourself.

Kim Newman

SPOILER ALERT!

Inevitably, a movie book of this ilk will contain spoilers. It also contains manners, though. As such, each entry starts with a list of the movies being talked about, so that you can bypass anything you've not yet seen. While there aren't huge spoilers, if there's a movie you want to remain completely spoiler-free on until you've seen it, simply skip that entry and read on to the next. Thanking you...

CLUES,
HAT TIPS AND
HIDDEN DETAILS

The opening credits of 1994's *Forrest Gump* seem like nothing more than a gentle introduction to a heart-warming drama. Against the background of Alan Silvestri's score, a feather drifts through the air, eventually landing between the feet of Tom Hanks's eponymous hero, who is sitting at a bus stop. The two-and-a-half minute sequence does the business of introducing key cast and crew while allowing time for the audience to settle down. But as soon as Forrest picks up that feather, the foreshadowing begins – the dirty running shoes, the table-tennis bat and the Bubba Gump Shrimp hat you glimpse inside his case are all hints about the story to come. Blink and you miss them.

Cinema loves its little clues – the signs of what lies ahead designed to reward the eagle-eyed. Look at the backdrop when Dame Judi Dench's name appears in the opening credits of *Skyfall* (2012) and you'll get a mighty clue as to what's in store. Likewise, the director of 2018's laptop-centric thriller *Searching* layered a whole host of hints to help unravel the movie's mystery in the smart opening montage. But such techniques are nothing new. The opening scenes of *The Wizard of Oz* (1939) are chock-full of little moments that herald later events. For example,

Zeke's transformation into the Cowardly Lion is suggested when he's asked: "You going to let a little old pig make a coward out of you?" And Hunk, who becomes the Scarecrow in Dorothy's dream, tells her: "Your head ain't made of straw, you know". Even the song "Somewhere Over the Rainbow" hints at the Technicolor that's about to transform Kansas into the land of Oz.

At times, though, such foreshadowing can be a little too overt. The opening credits of all the *Mission: Impossible* movies (like the TV show) include a montage of moments from the film itself. On the release of *Mission: Impossible – Fallout* (2018), some audience members grumbled about what they considered to be spoilers for the movie they had come to see. Mind you, nobody complained when the opening credits to horror hit *Final Destination* (2000) revealed how each character was going to die – probably because they were so subtle that no one noticed!

So, let's take a look at some of the best examples of foreshadowing, lines with a resonance that you might miss, hidden details that inform the plot, or just little things to look out for that add to the fun of watching a really good movie.

HUSH!

A Quiet Place *2018*

There's a brilliant piece of forewarning in the opening sequence of John Krasinski's 2018 breakout hit *A Quiet Place* – testament to the many little details that the movie gets right. The conceit of the film is that the surviving humans in a post-apocalyptic world must remain near-silent if they are to avoid a quick, brutal death at the hands of creatures with supernatural hearing. The audience isn't aware of this at the start, where we see Krasinski's character and his family gathering supplies in an abandoned shop. But there's a clue and a half there. The shop has been ravaged and very little remains...except tasty-looking potato chips. A stand full of the noisiest food in the world is there for all to see. This echoes nicely with the fact that when the film was released, many cinemas stopped selling loud snacks to viewers because so much of the film plays out in stone-cold silence.

WHAT'S IN A CHARACTER NAME?

Cast Away *2000*
The Wizard of Oz *1939*
Inception *2010*
The Empire Strikes Back *1980*

I n the 2000 movie *Cast Away* the leading character's name lends a big clue to what is coming. Tom Hanks plays Chuck Noland. C Noland. C-No-Land. Geddit? Interestingly, the movie was created in two chunks. The scenes before Hanks's character finds himself stranded on the desert island (see top right) were shot a year before the rest of the movie, when a trimmed-down, tanned Hanks was supposed to have been marooned for some time (see bottom right). The actor later said the physical transformation he underwent for the part may have contributed to his development of type 2 diabetes.

Other character names in films aren't shy of a few hints, either. Dorothy's surname in *The Wizard of Oz* is Gale – a clue to the tornado that whirls her away from Kansas. Christopher Nolan's *Inception* sees Ellen Page in the role of Ariadne. In Greek mythology, Ariadne is the princess who guides Theseus out of the Minotaur's labyrinth, so if you need to escape a maze or trap it pays to have an Ariadne on your team. This plays out heavily in the final act of *Inception*, where such skills come in really rather useful.

You still have to go some way to beat Darth Vader's foreshadowed revelation in *The Empire Strikes Back*. According to the film's writer and executive producer George Lucas, Darth is a variant of the word "dark", while Vader means "father" in Dutch. Darth Vader...Dark Father? One of the biggest plot twists in 1980s cinema was in plain sight all along...

LISTEN TO TEACHER

The Dead Zone *1983*
Hereditary *2018*

It pays to listen to teachers – especially in the movies. They have a habit of offering clues to where the plot of the movie you're watching is heading. Take 1983's *The Dead Zone*, for example. Christopher Walken plays the teacher in question, and at the start of the movie we see him reading a passage from Edgar Allan Poe's "The Raven". It's a dark poem, telling of a man who loses his lover and is then slowly driven mad by loneliness. This turns out to be a rough sketch of the teacher's story arc throughout the film.

And while we're in the classroom, let's take a lesson from 2018 horror movie *Hereditary*. In the school sequences, the teacher talks about Greek mythology and about how humans are pawns in the hands of the gods. The implication is that we're being manipulated by forces beyond our control – perhaps, even, into resurrecting a demon? Incidentally, for more foreshadowing in this movie, keep an eye on the miniatures that Toni Collette's artist character Annie (seen in the photo above) creates.

FROM THE KILLER'S MOUTH

Psycho *1960*

In Alfred Hitchcock's chilling classic *Psycho*, Anthony Perkins's Norman Bates is a man very much influenced by his mother. Listen to his dialogue on the subject early on and you'll hear an early clue about what's to come. When chatting to Janet Leigh's Marion about his mother, he describes her as "harmless as one of those stuffed birds". An innocent line? Absolutely not. By the end of the film his mother has met the same fate as one of those creatures.

Psycho's most famous scene, of course, includes a shower, a knife and a classic piece of Bernard Herrmann music. As realistic as the horror is in this memorable moment, rest assured that no humans were harmed in its making. The sound of that knife striking was actually made by plunging a blade into a melon. The melon did not survive the encounter.

BITING BACK AT CRITICS

Theatre of Blood *1973*
Gremlins 2: The New Batch *1990*

The late Vincent Price rated 1973's *Theatre of Blood* as a favourite among his vast filmography, and there's certainly an awful lot to like about the picture. Including, apparently, nearly 30 litres (about 7 gallons) of fake blood to create some extremely grisly murders. The story of an actor hunting down and murdering his critics probably appealed to those within the profession!

Theatre of Blood is far from the only film that takes aim at critics, but few do it as overtly as *Gremlins 2: The New Batch*, which smashes down the fourth wall by bringing in critic Leonard Maltin for a cameo. Maltin had been unenthusiastic about the original movie, so when it came to the sequel director Joe Dante persuaded him to repeat his criticisms of it as part of a sequence by the fictional Clamp Cable Network (the character of Daniel Clamp was in part a thinly veiled take-off of Donald Trump, pre-politics). In Maltin's sequence, the gremlins wreak their revenge on the critic for slamming their first film, although the scene cuts away before we see his final fate. Might have been safer to give it five stars, Leonard.

When he came to direct the screen adaptation of comic-book series *Dick Tracy* (shown left), Warren Beatty wanted to capture the feel of the original format. He didn't just want a panel-style editing approach, of the type Ang Lee later adopted for 2003's *Hulk*; he wanted his film to *look* like a moving comic strip. To achieve this, he limited himself to the use of just seven colours in the film – the same ones that the comic strip had to work with. To enhance that look, the camera was grounded as much as possible during filming. Cinematographer Vittorio Storaro explained that the plan was to not move the camera at all if possible, but rather to capture each scene within a fixed, non-moving frame.

The terrific 2015 horror movie *It Follows*, a metaphor for sexually transmitted diseases (STDs), also uses colour to make a point. Writer/director David Robert Mitchell uses the colour pink to signify the loss of innocence of main character, Jay, played by Maika Monroe. When we first see her she's wearing a pink dress, standing in her room, which itself is full of pink items. However, after she has sex a little way into the film, bringing a deadly threat in her direction, the colour pink is all-but-wiped from the film's palette. Jay is never seen in pink again.

PALETTE RESTRICTIONS

Dick Tracy *1990*
It Follows *2015*

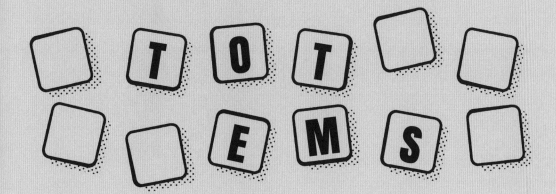

Inception *2010*

Christopher Nolan's *Inception* is a dense heist movie that definitely rewards a second viewing to pick up on all the clues and secrets you probably missed first time round. What's a dream and what isn't? And what about that ending, when Leonardo DiCaprio's character, Dom Cobb, sets his totem spinning on the table? In the film, characters use totems to work out whether they're in their own reality (either dreaming or awake), or in someone else's dream. For example, Cobb's partner Arthur's totem is a loaded red dice. If he rolls the dice and the weighting does its job, the same number will appear face up each time if he's not dreaming. If the dice acts in any way differently, he'll know that he *is* dreaming. So far so good.

Cobb's totem is a mini spinning top. If he spins it, and it keeps spinning, he'll know that he's dreaming. However, if it topples, as it should in the real world, he'll know he's awake. At the end of the movie, we see Cobb reunited with his children in some degree of a happy ending. When he spins his totem (see photo opposite), it keeps spinning...Or does it? Do we catch a glimpse of it stumbling a little? Hard to say – Nolan cuts the screen to black, puts up the title card and ends his film there. The director has a policy of not discussing his own interpretation of his movies, so we'll never know for sure whether Cobb is still dreaming or not. But perhaps the important thing is that Cobb doesn't seem to care one way or another – he spins his totem and then walks away from it, suggesting that he's stopped looking for reality, and instead just wants a relationship with his children again.

Just to throw in a little extra confusion, Michael Caine, who played Cobb's mentor, said that when he asked Nolan what was dream and what was reality, the director revealed that any scene with Caine in it was real...

WHAT'S IN THE LOGO?

Gremlins *1984*
Harry Potter *2001–11*
Scott Pilgrim vs. the World *2010*
Wreck-It Ralph *2012*
Frankenweenie *2012*
Raiders of the Lost Ark *1981*
A Very Brady Sequel *1996*

Warner Bros.'s iconic shield logo disappeared from its films at the end of the 1960s. It didn't return in earnest until 1984's *Gremlins*, when director Joe Dante – who has a huge love for old Warner Bros. classics – asked for it to be used in the film. His wish was granted, and you'll see it on almost all Warner Bros. films today.

One of the most subtle and effective uses of the logo can be seen in the *Harry Potter* collection. It's generally accepted that each of the eight Harry Potter movies gets gradually darker in terms of its story. To reflect this, the colour palette of the logo seen in each film's opening darkens slightly with each successive film in the series. This is only fully noticeable when you put them side by side. Start with *Harry Potter and the Philosopher's Stone* and you'll see blue sky and clouds behind the logo; by the time you get to the last film in the franchise, *Harry Potter and the Deathly Hallows Part 2,* the background is so dark it's difficult to make out the logo itself.

It's increasingly a trend for movies to create a take on a studio logo that reflects the film concerned. Both *Scott Pilgrim vs. the World* (Universal) and *Wreck-It Ralph* (Disney) transformed their parent companies' logos into blocky computerized versions, as if they'd been put together on a Super Nintendo. Disney, notoriously protective of its visual identity, even allowed composer Danny Elfman to tinker with the musical motif that opens the studio's films to create a more sinister version for Tim Burton's *Frankenweenie*. Plenty of filmmakers have also had fun matching the opening shot of a film to the Paramount mountain. Examples? Try *Raiders of the Lost Ark* and *A Very Brady Sequel*, both of which dissolve the logo card onto a scene showing a similar mountain top.

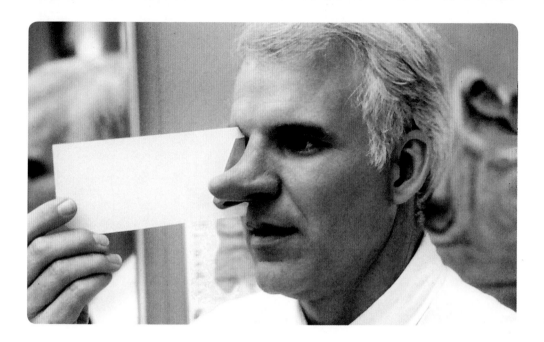

WHEN 25 EQUALS 20

Roxanne *1987*

Steve Martin wrote and starred in *Roxanne*, the acclaimed 1987 updating of the Cyrano de Bergerac story. Part and parcel of playing the lead role was the sizeable hooter that came with it. Martin wore a prosthetic nose during filming, which took some 90 minutes to put on and 2 minutes to take off. There's a point in the film (shown above) when Martin's character, C D Bales (a nod to the Cyrano de Bergerac source there), talks to a plastic surgeon, and he holds up a picture of the nose that he actually wants. The nose that appears in the photograph he is holding is, as it happens, Steve Martin's real-life nose!

The most celebrated scene in the movie, though, is where Bales is challenged to tell 20 nose jokes. Get counting when the scene starts and you'll realize that he actually tells 25. When he gets to 19 jokes in, he asks those around him what the running total is. They tell him, falsely, that he's done 14, and so he reels off another half dozen! However, viewers of the TV cut of the film got one joke less. You can tell which version you're watching when you get to the gag "Finally, a man who can satisfy two women at once". If you hear it, you're watching the cinematic cut, and get the full 25 jokes. If you don't, you're watching the edited-for-TV version, with only 24.

WHAT'S CAP BEEN MISSING?

Captain America: The Winter Soldier *2014*

The start of the second Marvel Captain America movie, *Captain America: The Winter Soldier*, sees the character of Steve Rogers familiarizing himself with everything he's missed out on following a decades-long sleep. He's put together a list, which we see in the movie. Thing is, the first five entries on that list differed based on where the film was released. In the UK, viewers learned that Rogers has missed The Beatles, the 1966 World Cup final, Sean Connery and the TV show *Sherlock*. American audiences saw a different list, which included entries for *I Love Lucy*, the Berlin Wall coming down, Apple's Steve Jobs and disco. Russian moviegoers saw Yuri Gagarin and the dissolution of the Soviet Union in 1991. In France? The 1998 World Cup, Daft Punk and *The Fifth Element*. And in South Korea, the *Dance Dance Revolution* video game, Ji-Sung Park and *Oldboy*.

SEEING RED

The Untouchables *1987*
Battleship Potemkin *1925*

The colour red is carefully used in Brian De Palma's 1987 hit *The Untouchables*. Viewers get the sense early in the film that Al Capone, played by Robert De Niro, is a gangster who doesn't necessarily do the dirty work himself. The face he shows wider Chicago is that of an ordinary businessman. Thus, the first time De Palma's camera takes us from the outside of the Lexington Hotel to the door of Capone's suite, the scene is awash with red – red carpets, red curtains, red wallpaper, red uniforms on the hotel staff...Symbolically, though, the red stops at the foot of Capone's bed, the implication being, of course, that to the outside world Capone doesn't indulge in violence himself.

Later, when Kevin Costner's Eliot Ness confronts Capone in his hotel, the exchange takes place on a staircase swathed in blood-red carpet and drapery, as Capone threatens someone who is outside his inner circle for the first time in the movie. The gangster is rattled, and the colour palette reflects that.

The Untouchables's most famous sequence is the staircase shootout at the station (see below left), an homage to the Odessa steps sequence in Sergei Eisenstein's 1925 *Battleship Potemkin* (see below). The seemingly incongruous sailors who ascend the stairs in De Palma's film are a deliberate nod to the movie he's honouring here.

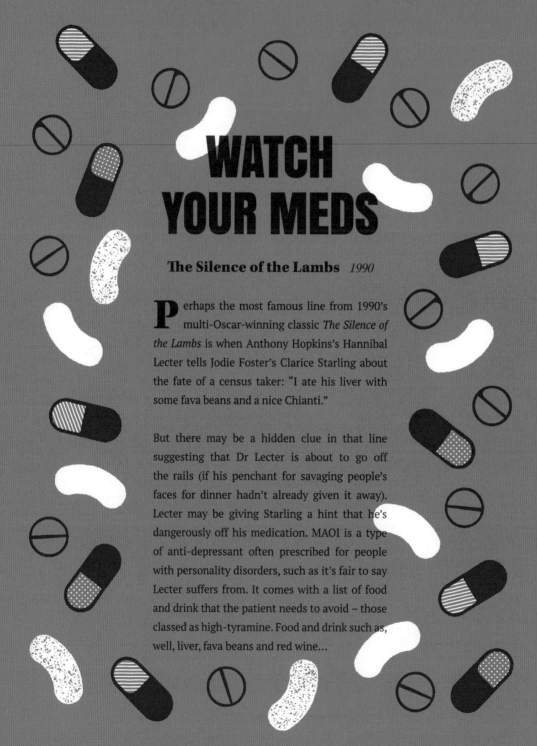

WATCH YOUR MEDS

The Silence of the Lambs *1990*

Perhaps the most famous line from 1990's multi-Oscar-winning classic *The Silence of the Lambs* is when Anthony Hopkins's Hannibal Lecter tells Jodie Foster's Clarice Starling about the fate of a census taker: "I ate his liver with some fava beans and a nice Chianti."

But there may be a hidden clue in that line suggesting that Dr Lecter is about to go off the rails (if his penchant for savaging people's faces for dinner hadn't already given it away). Lecter may be giving Starling a hint that he's dangerously off his medication. MAOI is a type of anti-depressant often prescribed for people with personality disorders, such as it's fair to say Lecter suffers from. It comes with a list of food and drink that the patient needs to avoid – those classed as high-tyramine. Food and drink such as, well, liver, fava beans and red wine…

SPLIT SCREEN

When Harry Met Sally... *1989*
Pillow Talk *1959*

A rguably the finest romantic comedy of the 1980s, *When Harry Met Sally...* was the result of the combined genius of Nora Ephron's pen and Rob Reiner's directing. In its most famous scene, Meg Ryan's character fakes an orgasm in the middle of a crowded restaurant, after which a woman at a nearby table (actually played by Reiner's mother, Estelle) says, "I'll have what she's having". It's pretty well known that Billy Crystal came up with that line during shooting, but this 1980s classic is packed with other "Did you know?" moments. For instance, the film features scenes of couples telling stories of their married life. Although these are actors performing, the tales they tell weren't scripted, but were real anecdotes that Reiner collected. (The little-seen 2018 comedy *Ideal*

Home pays some homage to this by showing a moving collection of real family photos from the albums of gay families over its end credits.)

The split-screen moments in *When Harry Met Sally...* (see above, top) were a tip of the hat to the Rock Hudson/Doris Day feature *Pillow Talk* (see inset photo above). In 1959, when that film was released, showing a couple in bed together was a no-no, so director Michael Gordon deployed the split-screen effect in order to show his two stars side by side and in bed – just different ones. Day would be on the phone in her room, Hudson sitting on the bed in his. Reiner used the technique to get across the idea that Harry and Sally were good friends rather than lovers.

THE CLUE IS IN THE SCORE

Total Recall *1990*
Interstellar *2014*

Total Recall was the first screen adaptation of Philip K Dick's short story "We Can Remember It for You Wholesale" – and remains the best to date. With Arnold Schwarzenegger on board it was never going to be anything less than a big, loud summer blockbuster, but this can't hide the air of mystery that lingers in the film courtesy of the questions it asks about what's real and what isn't. However, if you listen closely to Jerry Goldsmith's score (which the composer himself ranked as one of his best) you'll begin to realize that the music might well hide some answers to those questions. Look out for the melody that plays when the character of Quaid is dreaming, and each time it pops up you'll know that Schwarzenegger's character isn't experiencing reality at that moment.

For 2014's *Interstellar* (shown above), director Christopher Nolan allowed composer Hans Zimmer to come up with his own ideas for what he felt the sound should be. Ingeniously, Zimmer gives the audience a clue to enjoy on second viewing when Matthew McConaughey and his team land on their first planet, a water world (no Kevin Costner there, mind). The soundtrack when they arrive starts to incorporate a ticking noise, and it turns out that these ticks are one and a quarter seconds apart. Only when McConaughey's crew return to their ship does the significance of this become clear: each tick is a day of Earth time passing. Given that decades pass on that particular trip, that's an awful lot of ticks.

GUESS WHO TIPPED THE COPS OFF?

Reservoir Dogs *1992*

On its initial release, Quentin Tarantino's debut feature *Reservoir Dogs* left moviegoers puzzling over who shot Chris Penn's Nice Guy Eddie in the Mexican stand-off at the end. Tarantino was always insistent that the answer was in the frame, and when the movie got to home video and subsequent DVD releases, fans realized that was true. Mr White, played by Harvey Keitel, is the only one who gets to fire his gun twice. There's an error in the sequence, which Tarantino admitted but left in the film, where the special effect squib being worn by Penn went off a little too early. That's what makes the chronology of the shooting harder to work out.

One of the movie's other questions is which member of the gang ratted the others out to the police and caused the heist to go wrong. For this, Tarantino provides clearer clues. Look back to the breakfast scene at the start of the movie and that infamous conversation about tipping. When Lawrence Tierney's Joe wants to know which of the group hasn't left a dollar tip, it's Mr Orange (Tim Roth) who instantly lands Mr Pink in it. There's your first clue. If you want another, watch the scene where Nice Guy Eddie is heading back to the base of operations after the heist. His car is being followed by a balloon. The colour of that balloon? Orange. That's no coincidence.

WORKING OUT THE ENDING

The Usual Suspects *1995*
Once Upon a Time in America *1984*
Being There *1979*
Clue *1985*
Casablanca *1942*

Few endings leave themselves as much at the mercy of spoilers as Oscar-winning thriller *The Usual Suspects*, but in fact the huge twist is frequently foreshadowed throughout the movie. As the character of Verbal Kint is being interviewed, the objects around him and the noticeboard in the background provide a stream of clues that pretty much everyone misses on their first viewing – and can't miss on their second. Watch where his eyes settle throughout his interrogation, because he's usually looking at exactly the clue you need to figure out what's really going on.

Sergio Leone's epic *Once Upon a Time in America* is a classic example of a film with a deliberately ambiguous ending. The movie builds to a climactic moment in which James Woods's Bailey reveals a decades-old secret to Robert De Niro's Noodles. But Leone – who famously struggled to nail a final cut of the movie, trimming it at first down to eight hours before it reached its final, final cut of four –

worked extra hard to keep things vague. All we're allowed to see is the crunching jaws of a garbage truck. Is Bailey in there? Has he been killed? Only Sergio Leone ever really knew the answer, and the late, great director never told.

Hal Ashby's *Being There*, widely regarded as Peter Sellers's best ever screen performance, is another movie with an open ending. In it, we see the character of Chance walking on water – this apparently simple man suddenly becoming a metaphor for Christ, overturning perceptions of the character in the same way that *Forrest Gump* (1994) later did on its way to the Oscar podium.

As far as endings go, one of the most innovative ideas of the 1980s found its way into Jonathan Lynn's delightful comedy *Clue* (see opposite, top), based on the board game of the same name (Cluedo in the UK), which pulled the rug out from under moviegoers on its original release.

Its wheeze? Changing the ending depending on which screening people went to see. Three different endings were filmed and printed, and while subsequent home format releases brought them all together, in the cinema people either saw Miss Scarlett or Mrs Peacock committing the crime, or – in perhaps the most celebrated ending, with a huge tip of the hat to Agatha Christie – a denouement where everyone killed someone! The point where the versions diverge is when Wadsworth the butler, played by Tim Curry, reveals that he knows who the murderer is, explains the basics, then shuts off the electricity.

One of the most celebrated endings in cinema is that of *Casablanca* (shown below), with its famous line "Louis, I think this is the beginning of a beautiful friendship". But that's not the line that was actually spoken when the scene was shot. Those words came later, the brainwave of producer Hal B Wallis. Humphrey Bogart had to dub the line in after filming was complete. In fact, the script for *Casablanca* was in a state of flux right the way through filming anyway. It was unclear until very late into production whether Rick and Ilsa would end up together. A film that has a lot of fun with their romance, incidentally, is the spoof *Play It Again, Sam* (1972), written by and starring Woody Allen. It mirrors *Casablanca* as Allen's character looks to Bogart as his muse.

BACK TO THE PAST

Back to the Future Part II *1989*
Firefox *1982*
Back to the Future *1985*

T he opening credits of the first sequel to *Back to the Future* play over footage of clouds, as though the audience was flying through the air. As the titles end, the clouds segue into the opening of the movie proper, and we see the famous DeLorean negotiating a busy skyway. In fact, those clouds were reused footage, originally shot and used for Clint Eastwood's *Firefox* (1982). Five years later, the makers of *Back to the Future Part II* decided that footage would be just the job for their own movie – and would save them a few dollars in the process.

But that's not the only example of recycling in this film. The opening also replays the end sequence of 1985's *Back to the Future*, with some subtle changes. The character of Jennifer is now played by Elisabeth Shue rather than Claudia Wells and the dialogue is slightly different. For example, Marty drops the word "man" when he tells Jennifer "are you a sight for sore eyes". One or two pieces of footage from the first film are also reused, including the scene showing Crispin Glover's George and Lea Thompson's Lorraine standing together at their front door. The DeLorean landing and crashing into the bins is the same, as is Christopher Lloyd's Doc rummaging through the bin for fuel. Finally, the DeLorean backing up, ready for take-off, also came from the first film. The first entirely new scene for the second film comes nearly two minutes in, when Thomas F Wilson's Biff runs out of the house, and sees the car take off.

THERE ARE SIGNS

The World's End *2013*

The plot of *The World's End* (arguably director Edgar Wright's most underrated film) sees five old friends reunited for a pub crawl through their home town. The style of the signs inside each of the 12 pubs they visit, with their fake chalk writing, is identical – a comment on how homogenous many drinking establishments have become in the UK. More significantly, the names of the pubs foreshadow how the story will develop. For instance, the Famous Cock, the third stop on the group's travels, is a signpost of sorts for Simon Pegg's character, Gary King, who walks into the pub expecting to be recognized after being banned from the establishment many years before. Disappointingly, nobody bats an eyelid. Other stops include the Hole in the Wall, where a car comes crashing in, and the Trusty Servant, where the question is effectively posed as to who the character of Reverend Green is actually serving. And the meaning of the last stop, the World's End, can hardly be misunderstood...

One final thing to look out for. Toward the end of the film, a Cornetto wrapper floats into the shot. This is an obvious nod to the fact that the film is the concluding part of what has become known as the "Cornetto Trilogy", with previous films *Shaun of the Dead* (2004) and *Hot Fuzz* (2007) also being directed by Wright and co-written by Pegg.

ONCE UPON A TIME IN THE WEST

When Clint Eastwood declined the opportunity to make more "Man With No Name" movies, director Sergio Leone embarked on one final, hugely ambitious western. The result, *Once Upon a Time in the West* (1968), remains massively influential (the opening shot of Hill Valley in 1990's *Back to the Future Part III* is a direct homage, for a start). In fact, Leone stood on the shoulders of other westerns to make his masterpiece, and there are several factors that contribute to its distinct look and feel.

runs like clockwork in *High Noon*, Leone puts his three gunfighters in a bad mood by making the train they are waiting for two hours late.

1 The opening sequence pays particular homage to 1952's *High Noon* (also see page 176). But whereas everything

2 To get away from the studio-lot look and feel of westerns, Leone shot his on location. This accounts for the lack of gloss in his sets and settings – just look at how ramshackle the train track is for a start. Furthermore, the town in the film was built especially for the picture, just on location.

3 Leone's opening sequence is all about build-up and, unlike many classic westerns, when the shootout comes

it's quick and brutal. Two Kevin Costner westerns tip their hat to Leone's approach. The underrated 2003 film *Open Range* pays homage to the messy, ugly shootout, and Lawrence Kasdan's biopic *Wyatt Earp* (1994), in which Costner starred, builds up to a showdown at the OK Corral and then zips through it in double-quick time.

4 Charles Bronson's harmonica-playing character tends to deliberately slide into scenes, such as the one above where he's just been revealed by the train he was on pulling away. Throughout the film he's often shown in the distance, slightly obscured, or sliding in from the side of the frame.

5 One way to show the passage of time was with a fly slowly buzzing around actor Jack Elam (who, incidentally, appeared in *High Noon*). For this to work, his beard had to be smeared with jam, and a jar of flies kept in the vicinity. Eventually, one landed in the right place.

6 There's no music accompanying these stark shots. Ennio Morricone, who composed the superb score for the film, did put some ideas together but Leone decided to go with natural sounds only, as he felt they worked all the better to aid the slow, deliberate build-up and screw-turning tension.

WORKING AROUND PRODUCTION CHALLENGES

When Pixar or Walt Disney Animation Studios put together one of their feature films, they effectively make the movie time and time again before a frame of animation is completed. The films are storyboarded, played in rough form and edited in advance. The physical animation is the most intensive part of the process so problems are ironed out before a full crew puts it together. When Disney's movie *Tangled* (2010) was six months away from its release, its original director, Glen Keane, noted that 40 per cent of the animation work was still to be done. But at its core, the film had been built.

It's not an approach that always works, of course. Disney Animation always tries to include a hint about its next film in its features. Most notably, in 2016's *Zootopia* we see the character of Duke Weaselton selling a batch of pirated DVDs. Among his wares is a film called *Gigantic*. This animation, based on the story of Jack and the Beanstalk, was planned to be a Disney release called *Giants* in 2018, but the plug was pulled on the project in late 2017. That DVD cover in *Zootopia* is the only reference to the movie that ever made it to film. An extra nerdy fact for you: Duke Weaselton is voiced by Alan Tudyk and his character is a hat tip to the Duke of Weselton in *Frozen* (2012), who he also voiced.

Live action faces different challenges, of course. You can plan as carefully as you like, but if you head to the set and it's raining when your scene calls for sunshine, then you'll need your wits about you. Even films that seem flawless contain elements that are the result of decisions made on the spot. Robert Towne's script for *Chinatown* (1974), for instance, is widely regarded as a pretty perfect screenplay. But for Towne, it was the result of lots of gambles, of constant fights with director Roman Polanski, of trying things that didn't work. As Towne later admitted to filmmaker Brad Bird, he didn't really know what he was doing; he had no idea he was creating something that would be so revered.

And look again at 1988's *Die Hard*. Despite being a supporting character, Hart Bochner's Harry Ellis steals every scene. Yet the sleazy executive could have been so different. Director John McTiernan initially hated how Bochner was playing the character, and asked him to change it. Bochner persisted, but the only reason his interpretation of the character made it to the screen intact was because McTiernan spotted producers Lawrence Gordon and Joel Silver laughing their heads off while watching Bochner on a monitor. The director duly told his actor to carry on.

Here, then, is a whole bunch of movie-making moments that you might not expect. In some cases they reflect last-resort decisions. In others, an injury, an incident or just circumstances on the day of shooting took a film in a different direction to what its makers had planned.

LATE REDUBS AND CUTS

21 Jump Street *2012*
Spice World *1997*

T he successful film take on hit TV series *21 Jump Street* earned fan bonus points by sneaking the stars of the TV show into the movie for a cameo. Thus, we see Peter DeLuise and Johnny Depp as undercover DEA agents in the huge shootout at the end. That's a fairly obvious gag, though. A moment that makes slightly less sense comes in the scene where a drama teacher is regaling his class with an anecdote about his days as an actor, "doing cocaine with Willie Nelson's horse". The line that was spoken when the scene was shot was "doing cocaine with Whitney Houston's niece", but after Houston's tragic death in 2012, filmmakers decided to amend the line. The problem was, they weren't able to reassemble the cast and reshoot the scene, so the line would have to be changed using additional dialogue recording (ADR), which meant they had to find a sentence that exactly matched the movements of the actor's lips. The result was that Willie Nelson's horse gag.

It's worth noting that late changes to films to cover real-life events are not uncommon. For example, mentions of Gianni Versace and Princess Diana were cut out of *Spice World* very late in the day when both passed away just before the release of that film.

CLINT MOVES FAST

American Sniper *2014*

Clint Eastwood's gigantic 2014 hit *American Sniper* is a war movie starring Bradley Cooper which, in the midst of its sombre storytelling, contains a huge gaffe. It comes at the moment where Cooper's character, Chris Kyle (on whose real-life story the film is based), cradles his newborn daughter for the first time. This emotionally charged scene is undermined – to say the least – by the fact that this baby is obviously (and it took a lot of restraint not to use block capitals there) not real. It's not even *close* to looking real. Cooper later admitted on the *Ellen* show that he "couldn't believe that we were working with a plastic baby...I was just like, this is nuts".

The explanation at the time of the film's release was that the real baby planned for the scene got a fever. But Eastwood's directorial style is notoriously fast, and he doesn't like waiting around, so it's likely that his desire to keep up the momentum played a part in allowing the scene with the fake baby to stand. Eastwood rarely does more than two or three takes of a shot, and has been known to shoot and use rehearsals (notably the saloon sequence in 1992's *Unforgiven*). He wants the production of his films to keep moving, and they generally do.

QUIET BREAKTHROUGHS

Westworld *1973*
The Great Mouse Detective *1986*
Young Sherlock Holmes *1985*
King Kong *1933*

While some films are obvious forerunners for visual effects – *Star Wars* (1977), *TRON* (1982), *Terminator 2: Judgment Day* (1991) and *Jurassic Park* (1993) tend to hog the headlines – some less well-known movies have also proved pivotal when it comes to special effects.

Westworld, directed by the late Michael Crichton and an obvious forerunner of *Jurassic Park*, with similar themes, is not only a much-loved sci-fi film, but also a real pioneer in big-screen CGI. On a very tight budget, too. A man called John Whitney, Jr., with just $20,000 and four months to play with, put together the visual effect from the point of view of the gunslinger, played by Yul Brynner. The gunslinger's view is blocky and pixelated – at a time when computers were nowhere near able to render such an effect in the way they do now. This is still a digital effect, though, requiring individual colour separations of film, broken down into blocks, to be scanned and processed individually. It took months to complete, and takes up barely 30 seconds of screen time in the end. But it's regarded as the first full digital effects shot in a motion picture.

Arthur Conan Doyle's most famous creation, Sherlock Holmes, has inadvertently turned out to be at the heart of two visual effects breakthroughs. Toward the end of *The Great Mouse Detective*, we see the inner workings of London's Big Ben clock tower. This marks Disney's first ever mix of traditional characters and computer generated animation.

Young Sherlock Holmes, meanwhile, represents another milestone, with the character of the knight presented in the look of a stained-glass window. This was – for the first time in cinema – a fully computer-generated, photorealistic animated character (see right). The core work was done by John Lasseter, who later pioneered other animated breakthroughs with *Toy Story* (1995).

For major seismic shifts in special effects, though, 1933's *King Kong* is surely the greatest pioneer. This was in part down to the stop-motion animation work of Willis O'Brien (building on his ground-breaking success in 1925's *The Lost World*), but also its rear projection techniques (where actors work against a backdrop that's projected onto a screen behind them). It's as simple as it sounds, but *King Kong* was the moment where it was clear it could have massive impact. Look at the scene with Fay Wray's Ann Darrow in the tree in the foreground, while Kong and T-Rex scrap it out behind her (shown below). That's Wray reacting to the footage being screened before her eyes for real. Even better, the timing of the smoke bomb being thrown at the stegosaurus was so on the ball because the actors could see the footage right before them!

THE YANKEES FAN IN THE METS HAT

City Slickers *1991*

In the opening sequence to the comedy western *City Slickers*, New York Yankees fan Billy Crystal wears a New York Mets hat. It's something Crystal has confessed he's asked about a lot by fans of the movie. As it turns out, there were two reasons that he temporarily switched allegiance – and both came down to cash.

The story goes that Crystal had been trying to organize a Comic Relief Day at Yankee Stadium, involving himself, Whoopi Goldberg, Robin Williams and other notable actors. He had planned a day of activities and fundraising, but the Yankees declined the request. Their rivals, the Mets, not only said yes, but also made a heavy donation to the charity.

For the running of the bulls scene that kicks off *City Slickers* (see above), the original plan was for Crystal's character Mitch to wear a Yankees top and hat. But the Yankees refused to waive the $40,000 licensing fee for including their team-wear in the film. The Mets, however, did. This and the Mets's generosity during Crystal's fundraising sealed the deal – and that's how the costume decision was made.

TOM'S NOSE

Mission: Impossible III *2006*

Of the many visual effects in *Mission: Impossible III*, director J J Abrams's favourite involves an English character actor's sleeve and Tom Cruise's nose.

In a TED Talk in 2007, Abrams explained how he faced a problem during the filming of his directorial feature debut, when the needs of the story clashed with the comfort of his star. A scene called for Eddie Marsan's goon to insert a medical gun into Tom Cruise's character's nostril (for the purpose of injecting a micro-explosive into his brain, of course). The problem was, having a gun inserted into your nostril hurts like the dickens. When Marsan tried to do it gently, it didn't look right, and when he did it with the fervour expected of a supervillain's henchman, it hurt Cruise's nose. "I learned very early on in my career," said Abrams, "don't hurt Tom's nose."

He solved the problem with a bit of makeup and a borrowed costume sleeve. In the final film, the hand you see pushing the gun up Tom Cruise's nose belongs not to Eddie Marsan, but to Cruise himself.

WHY ASK PERMISSION?

The Florida Project *2017*
Escape From Tomorrow *2013*

For his Oscar-nominated drama *The Florida Project*, director Sean Baker based most of the story at the fictional Magic Castle motel, situated five or six miles away from Florida's Walt Disney Magic Kingdom theme park. For the film's finale he needed footage of the park, but he knew that Disney would never give him permission to shoot there (conversely, Disney's own *Saving Mr. Banks*, 2013, and *Tomorrowland*, 2015, were shot extensively in the company's theme parks). As such, Baker adopted a stealth approach, and used an iPhone and a skeleton crew to get the scenes he needed, aware that he'd be ejected from the premises if Disney worked out what was going on. He got what he needed, and that's the footage you see at the end of the film.

The independent *Escape From Tomorrow*, written and directed by Randy Moore, went a step further. Pretty much the entire film was shot without permission at Walt Disney World and Disneyland in Florida. The filmmakers managed this by using hand-held video cameras, similar to those used by tourists in the park, and by referring to copies of the screenplay on their phones instead of hard copies. Paranoid that Disney would hear about the project, Moore decamped to South Korea to complete post-production.

In the end, Disney made no comment on either *The Florida Project* or *Escape From Tomorrow*. But the truth is, the adage of "ask for forgiveness afterward rather than permission before" is one that filmmakers often live by.

EXTRAS ON A BUDGET

Four Weddings and a Funeral *1994*
Gandhi *1982*

Watch *Four Weddings and a Funeral* – the movie that kick-started Hugh Grant's career – and you'll see lots of small telltale signs that this was a low-cost project. The film had a modest production budget of under £3 million and, given the number of characters and locations involved, this required some creative thinking. Cost-cutting measures included having Rowan Atkinson's vicar officiating at two of the four weddings (see below) to avoid having to pay for another actor. Furthermore, the montage of pictures that plays at the end of the movie includes production crew, again to keep costs down. Something else to look out for: one of the extras in the film is the British politician Amber Rudd. In lieu of payment, she was listed in the end credits as "Aristocracy Coordinator".

On the flipside, Richard Attenborough found he had no shortage of extras when he was filming *Gandhi* in India. After a call for people to take part in the funeral sequence was put out in the local press, more than 300,000 people turned up. Some 18 cameras were required to capture the scene, which lasted just over 2 minutes in the finished movie (notably shorter than any of Attenborough's – much-deserved – awards acceptance speeches). It remains a world record for extras in a movie, and it's hard to imagine that it will ever be beaten now, in our more CG-driven world.

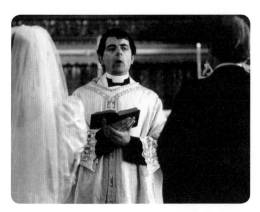 

A BIT OF BED REST

Carry On Doctor *1967*

From the early days of the *Carry On...* movies, a regular ensemble began to form. One of the key players in that familiar cast was Sid James – the man with the wrinkled face and a cackle that no one has ever managed to match. However, in early 1967, while filming the second season of the British TV show *George and the Dragon*, James suffered a near-fatal heart attack. He spent three weeks in an oxygen tent, and only gradually recovered.

James's health cost him the lead in *Follow That Camel* (1967), for which Phil Silvers stepped into his shoes. But director Gerald Thomas was desperate that James wouldn't be absent from the line-up for more than one film. So, he came up with a plan to make sure James could be in the next one. *Carry On Doctor* was shot in September 1967 and released in December of that year. In it, the still-recovering James played the role of Charlie Roper (shown above) – a patient confined to bed for the duration of the movie.

ON TRACK

School of Rock *2003*

L ed Zeppelin decline the vast majority of requests to use their music in feature films, so the appearance of their track "Immigrant Song" in *School of Rock* is noteworthy. As it turns out, there's a story behind it. Director Richard Linklater and star Jack Black were both aware of the bands attitude towards the use of their songs in cinema so they hatched a plan to persuade them. Linklater filmed a special clip (which can be seen on the DVD release), showing Black in front of a thousand fervent Led Zep fans requesting that the song be used in the movie. The band acquiesced.

Two more things to watch for. Black plays two different roles in the film. His main character is aging guitarist Dewey Finn, but he also has to impersonate the character of Ned Schneebly. The clue to who he is at any particular time lies with his hair: his parting switches sides depending on his character. Also, if you want a quick snapshot of the power of product placement in the movies, note how every parent in the film drives a Volvo.

THE INJURED MOVIE STAR

Indiana Jones and the Temple of Doom *1984*
The Fugitive *1993*
Dr. Strangelove or: How I Learned to Stop Worrying and Love the Bomb *1964*

Director Steven Spielberg once said that he made 1989's *Indiana Jones and the Last Crusade* by way of recompense for *Indiana Jones and the Temple of Doom*, a movie he regretted for its darkness and violence (this, along with *Gremlins*, 1984, would lead the Motion Picture Association of America (MPAA) to introduce the harder PG-13 rating, to supplement the softer PG). *Temple of Doom* may not exactly be wholesome family entertainment (the chilled monkey brains are a decent litmus test for whether you can stomach it), but in fact it has lots to recommend it.

One of the most notable things you might spot on a re-watch, though, is that you don't see the face of leading man Harrison Ford too much during the film's action sequences. The reason is that while shooting one of the movie's big fight scenes,

Ford suffered a bad back injury that worsened as filming progressed (he later said that having to ride elephants didn't help the situation). With production scheduled to move to sets in the UK, Ford was flown back to the USA for treatment and the film faced a two-month shutdown.

But then in stepped Ford's stunt double – and the film's stunt expert – Vic Armstrong. For the next few weeks, Armstrong shot Ford's scenes, and it was only later, when the star was fit enough to return, that the close-up shots were added. However, Armstrong seems to have worked above and beyond what was strictly necessary. Look carefully at when the captured kids are released, the moments involving the mine car and the fight on the conveyor belt, and you'll see that it's Armstrong playing the hero, not Ford.

It was a different case with *The Fugitive*. Yes, that certainly is Harrison Ford you see throughout the movie, but the decision for his character, Dr Richard Kimble, to walk with a limp came about after Ford sustained ligament damage when shooting the chase sequence in the woods. Thankfully, those scenes were chronologically early in the film so Kimble's limp seems natural for the rest of the story.

In another example of on-set injury, Peter Sellers badly damaged his ankle during the filming of *Dr. Strangelove or: How I Learned to Stop Worrying and Love the Bomb*. As a result, Sellers had to give up playing the character of Kong (although given the multitude of characters he was already playing, audiences were hardly short-changed), and Slim Pickens took on the role. The character of Strangelove is in a wheelchair (see above) for the duration of the feature because of that injury.

RAMIFICATIONS AND REACTIONS

The Manchurian Candidate *1962*
Dirty Harry *1971*
Das Boot *1981*
The Birds *1963*
Alien *1979*
The Godfather *1972*

Sometimes, a stunt doesn't quite go to plan, and leaves the actor involved with lasting damage that can have a knock-on effect...

Go back to the original version of *The Manchurian Candidate* and watch the scene in which Frank Sinatra fights Henry Silva. As Sinatra smashes through the table he actually breaks his little finger. It sounds like a small injury, but it had a fairly immediate impact on an iconic role. Sinatra had been all set to take on the title role in *Dirty Harry*, but this injury was apparently one of the reasons why he had to drop out of the film. If Sinatra hadn't fallen, Clint Eastwood would never have had one of his most famous characters. Then again, *The*

Dead Pool (1988) might never have been made. Swings and roundabouts.

The German submarine thriller *Das Boot* – a film that started as a TV series before being edited for feature movie release – worked around an on-camera injury to Jan Fedder. Again, this was a case when an actor's role was rewritten pretty much on the fly, to confine his character to bed for part of the movie. Incredibly, the dramatic sequence where Fedder sustained his broken ribs made it to the film. Watch him fall off the bridge of the submarine, and you'll hear one of his fellow actors immediately say "man overboard". Director Wolfgang Petersen thought this was an improvisation and liked it, before realizing that the actor was indicating that Fedder was in real trouble.

Also real is the ending of *The Birds*, where Tippi Hedren fends off the huge flock of birds. Director Alfred Hitchcock had promised that the birds would be mechanical – and that was what Hedren was expecting. But Hitchcock, renowned for being ruthless with his actors, wanted a genuine reaction, and used live birds instead. Hedren was petrified, and the blood the birds drew was real.

You get real blood for your money in *Alien*, too. Director Ridley Scott had prepared his actors for the infamous chestburster shot, where we see the infant xenomorph erupt from John Hurt's chest (see right). However, he neglected to tell them that the blood they were going to be spattered with was real. The shock you see in the scene, not least on the face of Veronica Cartwright, is oh-so-real.

One more bloody story, this time concerning *The Godfather*. Arguably the most famous scene in the film is the one in which film producer Jack Woltz, played by John Marley, wakes up next to the head of his horse (see right). It's a shocking, iconic sequence, and the reaction from Marley in the scene is completely genuine. Director Francis Ford Coppola swapped the prop head they had been planning to use for the head of a real horse obtained from a local slaughterhouse. Unsurprisingly, there was a significant public backlash when this detail was revealed.

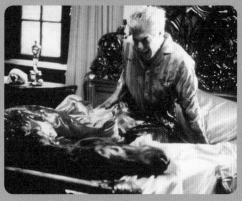

A FAMILIAR DANCE

Beauty and the Beast *1991*
Sleeping Beauty *1959*

The exquisite dance sequence between Belle and the Beast in Disney's animated classic *Beauty and the Beast* is rightly lauded for both its emotional and its technical impact. Part of it is, in fact, the first feature film work by Pixar, back in the days before it joined the Disney empire. (*Toy Story*, Pixar's first full length movie, was still some four years away.)

But that's not the main point of note about the dance. For how do you put a brilliantly choreographed but animated dance on screen? How can you get the steps right and make sure it all looks authentic? Well, Disney managed it by reusing the choreography from a previous movie. The filmmakers repurposed the dance between Princess Aurora and Prince Phillip in *Sleeping Beauty*. The steps between Aurora and Phillip were recreated one by one, so the dances in the two films are identical even though the dancers are different.

CARY'S NUDGE

North by Northwest *1959*

Regarded by some as Alfred Hitchcock's masterpiece, *North by Northwest* (shown above) was an exciting, fast-moving blockbuster at a time when blockbuster movies weren't called anything of the sort. Hitchcock was still working with analogue filmmaking techniques which, of course, he used in innovative ways. But look out for the moment when Cary Grant is in the back of a police car, and the age-old technique of a screen behind the car is being used to simulate movement. There's a point at which not all the actors are going with it – until Grant gives the officer he's sitting next to a very overt nudge.

GET OFF MY LAWN!

Friday *1995*

When filming on location in residential areas, movie-makers have to hope for the cooperation and permission of the local residents. But they don't always get it. That was the case in the hit comedy *Friday*, where one local resident refused to move when the film was trying to capture a moment in his neighbourhood. Director, F Gary Gray, decided to carry on regardless and as such there's a brief moment in the film where you can spot a grumpy man on his lawn, pretty much staring toward the camera in the background.

MATCHING TWINS

Zodiac *2007*
The Social Network *2010*

Director David Fincher is one of the more subtle users of visual effects. *Zodiac* – perhaps his most underrated film – is the compelling story of the hunt for the Zodiac killer in 1970s San Francisco. In it, according to an exhaustive examination of Fincher's work by Kristian Williams, you'll find more visual effects shots than you will in Gareth Edwards's *Godzilla* (2014)! One example is the opening murder, in which all of the blood is a visual effect. There's not a drop of "real" (fake!) blood in view.

Perhaps the most compelling example of Fincher's use of effects to play with character comes in *The Social Network*. The Winklevoss twins are played by Armie Hammer and Josh Pence, who worked together for the best part of a year to get across the mannerisms of twin brothers. Fincher, of course, wanted them to look alike, too, so Hammer's face was digitally edited over Pence's. Thus, whenever you see the Winklevi (as screenwriter Aaron Sorkin famously called them) in the movie, you'll see Hammer's face on both of them, but the bodies of two different actors.

HERO IN A TIGHT SPACE

Batman *1989*
Batman Returns *1992*

Tim Burton's pair of Batman films are highly unusual when compared to modern superhero and comic-book movies. The reason? They were almost entirely shot on a studio lot.

The original *Batman* was filmed on a lot in London; *Batman Returns* (shown below) on one in Los Angeles. The only location shots were those that showed the exteriors of Wayne Manor. Everything else had to deal with the physical confines of a studio set. This proved particularly difficult on *Batman Returns*, as the temperature had to be kept low to accommodate the numerous live penguins that featured in the film (among the equally numerous overtly fake ones).

You get a real feel for the limited space when watching the Batmobile sequences. In real life, the car itself struggled to hit 40 mph, but this was tricky when trying to shoot car sequences in such limited space. Car chases are routinely shot with the camera low, to give the impression that cars are moving faster than they are. Burton used a mix of techniques to "increase" the speed of the Batmobile, but careful viewing will reveal that the car never really goes very fast.

MORE PAIN...

Mission: Impossible – Fallout *2018*
Patriot Games *1992*
The Passion of the Christ *2004*
Inglourious Basterds *2009*
City Heat *1984*
Syriana *2005*

The injury Tom Cruise sustained on the set of *Mission: Impossible – Fallout*, breaking his ankle while jumping from one building to the next (see opposite, top), is all the more remarkable given that the key moment remains in the finished movie. But it's not the only real-life injury that made it into the final cut.

Sean Bean picked up a permanent scar while filming a fight with Harrison Ford in *Patriot Games*. Ford hits Bean with a boat hook, cutting the actor above his eye. Bean carries the scar to this day.

Jim Caviezel, meanwhile, certainly suffered when taking on the role of Jesus in Mel Gibson-directed *The Passion of the Christ*. Not only was

he struck by lightning (off-camera) during the production of the movie, but one of the scenes where we see Christ being lashed went slightly wrong. To make the moment look realistic, real whips were used – the idea of course being that they wouldn't actually strike Caviezel's body. Unfortunately one of them did, causing an extensive wound on the actor's back.

Toward the end of Quentin Tarantino's *Inglourious Basterds*, we see Diane Kruger's character in the film, Bridget von Hammersmark, being strangled to death (see inset photo opposite). If it all looks frighteningly realistic it's testament in part to Kruger's acting but also to the fact that she genuinely passed out as a result of filming the scene (there was no lasting

damage). Incidentally, those hands around her neck belong to Tarantino himself.

The late Burt Reynolds's career pretty much derailed for two years after the filming of a sequence with Clint Eastwood on the set of *City Heat*. Again, this is a moment you can see in the film itself. In a scene that was completed on the first day of shooting, Reynolds is hit over the head with a chair. It was supposed to be a special stunt chair, which would collapse on impact. However, Eastwood picked up a metal chair by mistake and delivered Reynolds a direct blow. He was able to continue with filming only thanks to some strong painkillers to alleviate the blinding headache and the ringing in his ears. In his autobiography, Reynolds admitted that he felt he ruined the movie, and it took years for him to shake off the impact of the injury, causing him to drop out of the Hollywood limelight.

George Clooney, who took home an Oscar for his work in the film *Syriana*, is still paying the price for making it. There's a sequence in the movie where his character is tortured, and the torturer smashes the chair he is sitting in. As the chair, and Clooney, came crashing down, the actor smashed his head directly on the floor. Clooney spent a week in hospital as doctors tried to find the cause of the unbearable headaches he was experiencing. They eventually discovered leaking spinal fluid and treated the injury, but Clooney apparently still feels the ramifications of the incident.

THE LATE POST-CREDITS SEQUENCE

The Avengers *2012*
Big Hero 6 *2014*

The post-credits sequence for *The Avengers* came together very, very late in the day, and required some nimble scheduling work for the cast. This is the scene where the assorted heroes are sitting around a dinner table having a chunter. The idea for the extra sting came from dialogue that had been written for Robert Downey, Jr., to beef up the moment where Iron Man falls back to Earth at the end of the movie. The added dialogue, discussing a food place a few streets down, inspired the extra scene. By the time it came to filming this sequence, however, Chris Evans had grown a beard and had to wear a special cover to hide it. Watch the scene and you'll see he's the only one not given anything to eat.

Disney's Oscar-winning animated hit *Big Hero 6* pushed things even more to the wire. The film began its rollout in cinemas in the winter of 2014, but as late as July of the same year, its surprise post-credit didn't exist, and there were no plans to

include it at all. It was only when the filmmakers saw that year's *Guardians of the Galaxy* that they realized they needed to scramble something together. So, they had a brainstorming session, which led to the extra sequence being conceived in August and locked down with score in October. It really is the late Stan Lee doing the voice, too. The Marvel legend agreed to do the recording and in doing so made good on the teases that the film had already included, such as the pictures on the wall of Fred's mansion.

PRACTICAL INGENUITY

The Thing *1982*

Rob Bottin, then still in his early twenties, took on an extraordinary amount of work when he agreed to create the practical effects for John Carpenter's *The Thing*. His designs for a shape-shifting alien capable of killing and replacing its victims required dozens of effects shots and some ingenious mixtures of latex, animatronics and other in-camera trickery. Indeed, after months of working long hours and even sleeping on the floor of his workshop, Bottin eventually became so exhausted that he briefly wound up in hospital.

In his absence, Bottin hooked in another effects wizard, Stan Winston, to take up the slack. While the vast percentage of the creature effects you see in the final cut were created by Bottin, Winston's contributions can be spotted in a handful of shots. For instance, in the sequence where we see a dog slowly revealing its hideous alien form, there's a fairly tight shot of the beast as it's hit by shotgun blasts. This grotesque puppet was crafted at Stan Winston's studio. The end credits carry a special thanks to Winston for his assistance on the film.

One other thing to watch out for in *The Thing* – and a testament to the ingenuity involved in making the movie – is the helicopter. The production only had access to one chopper, but the story required two, to cover both the Norwegian and American bases. The solution? Paint that one helicopter differently on each side. Of course this meant it could only be shot flying in one direction for the Americans and the other for the Norwegians.

DETAILS, CHOICES AND MOMENTS

If you want to unravel the mystery of a film, it's worth paying close attention to its earlier stages. For there will often be clues, little bits of foreshadowing, and small choices that can offer a glimpse as to the tone and direction of a particular story.

An obvious example is M Night Shyamalan's Oscar-winning monster hit, *The Sixth Sense* (1999). Shyamalan, in that film in particular, is very careful in how he lays his clues. He makes small choices throughout that you can spot more clearly on a second viewing. While not wanting to give away one of history's most-given-away endings, you need to watch out for the colour red throughout the film. Any moment where you see red in the movie – and it took a lot of work to eradicate it from every other frame – there's a sizeable clue as to the direction in which the story is heading. Shyamalan was apparently obsessive on set about removing any unnecessary instances of the colour red in the sight of his cameras.

A film also drenched in spectacular use of red – watch how it's used to link two particular characters, for instance – is Nicolas Roeg's stunning *Don't Look Now* (1973). But in this instance, the film in particular uses editing techniques that are unsettling now, and were flat-out revolutionary at the time of the movie's release. These techniques offer a foreshadowing of what's to come and, as many have noted, if you pay close enough attention, you can work out just where the film is going within the first 20 minutes.

These two films are not alone. Beyond the current craze for Easter eggs in films – you'll find a Mickey Mouse hiding in pretty much every modern Disney movie, for instance – there are productions where there's something a lot deeper going on.

That's what we're going to look at in this chapter. The small, clever choices that offer us extra clues, the little details in the background, and the moments you may miss first time around, but will spot them every time after...

IT'S IN THE LYRICS

Beauty and the Beast *1991*

Disney's Oscar-winning animated hit *Beauty and the Beast* quickly won universal acclaim on its original release, and much credit went to its terrific score and songs. These were the work of lyricist Howard Ashman and composer Alan Menken, who had previously collaborated on Disney's *The Little Mermaid* (1989) and the original musical of *Little Shop of Horrors* (1986). Right up to the night of *The Little Mermaid's* Oscar wins, though, Ashman held back a secret: he was dying. He had contracted AIDS, at a time when the disease was deemed a death sentence.

The production of *Beauty and the Beast* was increasingly working around him as his illness took hold, and there's been much discussion about the resonance of some of the lyrics he wrote, in particular for "The Mob Song". This is the number where a crowd of villagers, whipped up by antagonist Gaston, head off to a castle to kill a beast, about which they know nothing other than what they've heard from rumours and scaremongering. "We don't like what we don't understand, in fact it scares us," they sing. "And this monster is mysterious at least."

A metaphor for AIDS? We'll never know for certain: Ashman tragically passed away at the age of 40, months before the film was complete. His sister discounts the theory that the song was related to his illness, although *Beauty and the Beast* producer Don Hahn – who completed and released a documentary about Ashman, *Howard*, in 2018 – described the song as "almost a metaphor" for what he was going through.

CAN WE GET ANOTHER TAKE OF THAT?

Dragon Lord *1982*
City Lights *1931*

Some scenes are so complicated and detailed that they require a fair few takes to get in the can. In this regard, few can claim the difficulties experienced by martial arts movie *Dragon Lord*, directed by and starring Jackie Chan. The film is said to hold the record for the most number of takes for a single scene – a total that apparently reached more than a thousand. No one has ever revealed exactly what sequence this was, but it's a fair bet that it was the physically demanding shuttlecock (jianzi) scene, which took around 40 days to film.

Chan isn't the only perfectionist director. In *City Lights*, there's a moment (shown left) where Charlie Chaplin's co-star, Virginia Cherrill, asks the simple question, "Flower, sir?" Chaplin, who also directed, reportedly demanded nearly 350 takes of the scene before he was happy. And this was a silent movie!

BLACK AND WHITE

Schindler's List *1993*
Some Like It Hot *1959*

The decision to film a movie in black and white is usually one of commerce – box-office returns for modern black-and-white films tend to be lower than colour ones. Should the subject come up, a studio will often ask that a movie is shot in colour even if it's destined to be released in black and white. This gives the studio options later on if required (for a DVD release, for example).

When it came to shooting his haunting classic *Schindler's List*, however, Steven Spielberg wasn't having any of that. He wanted the black-and-white pictures to be true and argued that converting from colour would give the image a pinkish tinge. The studio put up a fight, but after several weeks of to-ing and fro-ing Spielberg emerged the victor, enabling him to fulfil his vision of bringing to the screen the look and feel of a life without light.

In 1959, back in the days when black-and-white movies were still common, Billy Wilder was offered the option of filming *Some Like It Hot* in colour. Marilyn Monroe was reportedly annoyed when, after doing some test work in colour, Wilder opted for black and white after all. However, Monroe was won over when the director showed her the results of the tests he'd done and she saw for herself how the colour made Jack Lemmon and Tony Curtis look in their female get-up, which was...well...decidedly unconvincing. Black and white was the only way the film would work.

EMPTY FRAMES

Harold and Maude *1971*

Hal Ashby's glorious dark comedy *Harold and Maude* cast Ruth Gordon as the septuagenarian Maude. Unfortunately, Gordon couldn't drive, so the scenes where we see her behind the wheel of a hearse were carefully shot in order to conceal the fact that the car was being towed.

There's more to this film, though. Keep an eye out for the empty frames in the background in Maude's home. This is a nod to a suggestion in Colin Higgins's companion novel that Maude is suffering from some form of dementia. There's no overt expression of this in the movie – a scene where Maude explains that her memory isn't what it had been was never used – but those poignantly pictureless frames may set viewers wondering.

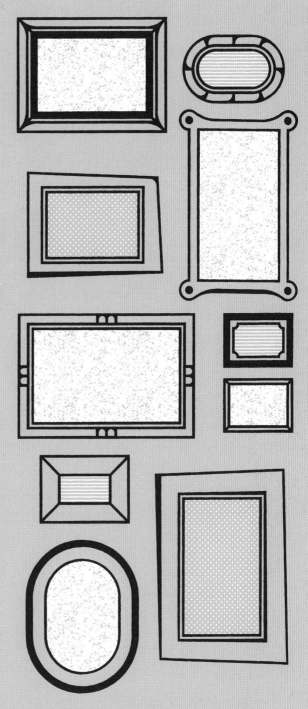

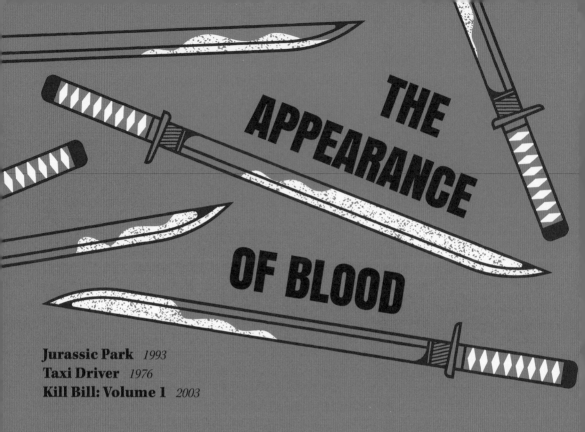

THE APPEARANCE OF BLOOD

Jurassic Park *1993*
Taxi Driver *1976*
Kill Bill: Volume 1 *2003*

The Motion Picture Association of America (MPAA) has often come into conflict with filmmakers over ratings, and blood is one of the most common reasons that they clash. Knowing this, producers and directors will consider carefully how they present blood on screen.

Steven Spielberg wanted *Jurassic Park* to get a clean PG rating in the UK and a PG-13 in the US. Removing blood from the equation was key to that, which is why you won't see a drop of it in the film, despite all those bloodthirsty dinosaurs.

Martin Scorsese faced a tough job getting *Taxi Driver* past the censors because of the amount of blood he'd included. Eventually, he compromised by taking some of the red out of the blood in the film's final shootout. That's why the scene has a slightly desaturated look (see picture comparison opposite). It worked: the film finally got its R rating.

A final bloodless fact: the MPAA doesn't normally allow the red stuff in trailers. Watch the trailer for *Kill Bill: Volume 1*, for example, and you'll see that the stains covering Uma Thurman's yellow outfit are black (they're red in the film itself). Keeping the MPAA happy and giving the film a broader marketing span were the reasons why this was changed for the trailer.

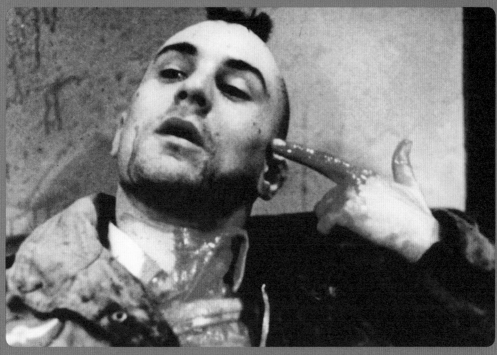

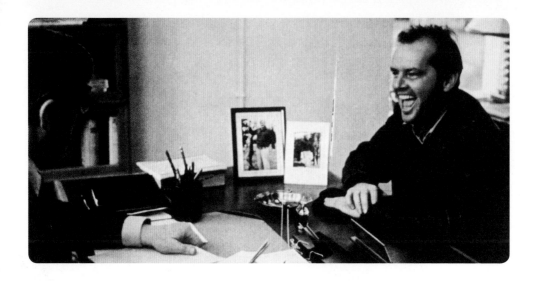

WHO NEEDS ACTORS?

Full Metal Jacket *1987*
One Flew Over the Cuckoo's Nest *1975*

When planning his Vietnam War film *Full Metal Jacket* – a movie shot entirely in the UK, with London's Isle of Dogs serving as a location for the battlefield – Stanley Kubrick brought Marine corps drill instructor R Lee Ermey on board as a technical advisor. However, as it happened, Ermey impressed Kubrick so much that he won the role of Gunnery Sergeant Hartman, which had been earmarked for Tim Colceri (Colceri got the smaller role of Doorgunner). Throughout filming, Ermey was known for improvising much of his dialogue.

There are other examples of bringing in a non-actor to play a scene. Namely in the Oscar-winning *One Flew Over the Cuckoo's Nest*.

The opening scene (see above) shows Jack Nicholson's character, Randle McMurphy, being admitted to the mental institution and meeting the man in charge of the facility, Dr John Spivey, played by Dean Brooks. What's interesting is that Brooks was not an actor; he was the real superintendent of the facility in Salem, Oregon, where the movie was being shot. When it came to filming the scene, Brooks wasn't given a script. Instead, he was handed a dossier on McMurphy and told to act as if this was a real patient he was meeting for the first time. Nicholson was briefed on where the scene ultimately needed to go, but Brooks was given the report and basically told to do his job. Watch it again, and you'll notice Nicholson quietly guiding it.

WOVEN TIMELINES

Dunkirk *2017*

Christopher Nolan's *Dunkirk* tells the real-life story of a daring rescue mission – the evacuation of over 300,000 Allied troops from northern France near the start of World War II. The film runs for 106 minutes, with three storylines woven together, as we see rescue efforts for air, sea and "mole" (another name for a pier). Having several storylines in a film isn't unusual, but what's particularly clever here is the way the three timelines are presented.

The stories are edited together in a way that makes it feel like they're running in parallel, but that's not the case at all. Viewers get their first clue about this right at the start of the film, when cards flash up on screen explaining that the air rescue takes an hour, the sea rescue a day, and the mole rescue a week. It's easy to overlook them as they seem like ordinary information cards to set the scene, but what they say is crucial to the chronology of the film. As the story progresses, these timelines gradually converge – even though it appears otherwise. Just to add to the confusion, after the point of convergence they separate again! At the end, we see evacuated troops on a train home, even as Tom Hardy's pilot is still trying to land his plane. So a word to the wise: read those cards and remember what they say.

THE LOOK OF JOY AND SADNESS

Inside Out *2015*

The emotion characters in Pixar's extraordinary animated film *Inside Out* are identified by some simple, effective colour coding. Notably, each personified emotion (Anger, Disgust, Joy, Fear and Sadness; see below, left to right) has his or her own distinct eye, skin and hair colour. There's one exception to this: the character of Joy. Joy is primarily yellow (she wears a green dress), but she has blue hair – the same colour as the character of Sadness. This is a deliberate nod to the film's key theme – the idea that in order to feel joy, one must also experience sadness. She is perhaps the most human of the emotions, in look, mannerisms and behaviour.

THE PASSAGE OF TIME

Groundhog Day *1993*

In the comedy classic *Groundhog Day*, weatherman Phil Connors (played by Bill Murray) finds himself reliving the same day over and over. In the film, we see him enduring 38 days in all, but it's been theorized that the story actually covers up to – and possibly more than – 10,000 days, and that the movie only shows a minuscule fraction of them. If that's true, it would be the same amount of time it would take Phil to become an accomplished pianist, a native French speaker and an ice sculptor, all from scratch. The film's late director, Harold Ramis, reckoned the timespan of the film is actually ten years. That's ten years we see Phil stuck in the same day, over and over.

Incidentally, the film's relatively bleak look (at least in weather terms) was chosen because it was the easiest to recreate when the scene needed to be repeated again and again and...

BEWARE TRANSLATIONS...

Anchorman: The Legend of Ron Burgundy *2004*

S o stuffed with jokes was *Anchorman: The Legend of Ron Burgundy* that, come the DVD release, it had an unusual extra feature: an entire additional movie, pieced together from material that didn't make the final cut of the main film. Even so, the cinema version is hardly shy of background jokes, one of which suggests that not every sign in a film is saying what you may think. For example, the Mexican restaurant that goes by the name *Escupimos en su Alimento*, emblazoned in big bright letters, isn't as welcoming as it may seem. The name means "we spit in your food". Beautifully, this isn't ever explained – it's just a delicious background gag.

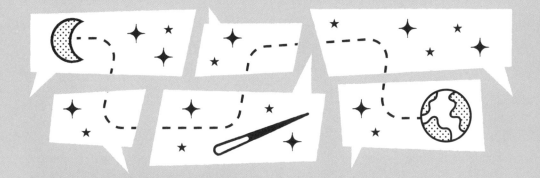

NECESSARY TECHNO-BABBLE

Apollo 13 *1995*

Ron Howard's dramatization of the nearly-ended-in-tragedy *Apollo 13* moon mission contains an awful lot of technical dialogue that, to many of us, doesn't make too much sense. But this was a deliberate choice. Howard was keen for his film to be as authentic as possible – and that meant technobabble. Listening to it, we really feel that the folk at mission control know what they're talking about, even if we don't. That's probably because the vast bulk of the dialogue was the real deal; most of the chatter between the *Apollo 13* crew and the team on the ground in Houston was taken from recordings of the conversations that really took place at the time.

FIRST CONTACT

Labyrinth *1986*

In a lovely, subtle piece of foreshadowing, Jim Henson's beloved movie *Labyrinth* gives viewers a small taste of what's to come right at the start of the film. Dotted around the bedroom of the character of Sarah (played by future Oscar-winner Jennifer Connelly), are small versions of some of the creatures that she meets later on in the film. There's also a copy of Maurice Sendak's book *Outside Over There*, the story of a girl who heads into a fantasy world to save her baby sister after she's kidnapped by goblins. Sound familiar? Quite. In the movie's end credits, Henson acknowledges his "debt to the works of Maurice Sendak".

DEBUTING AS JAMES BOND

Live and Let Die *1973*

The first line ever spoken by Roger Moore as the character of James Bond comes, of course, in *Live and Let Die*. But those first utterances didn't quite go as planned. In fact, it took 14 days of shooting before he said a line of dialogue that made it to the final cut. The words to listen out for are "Hello Felix, what are you doing here?" They are not the first words that we hear Moore say in the film, but the first he actually shot. Even then, he turned up on set only to discover that the day and a half of dialogue he'd learned had been cut back to just those seven words!

Actually, the first words Bond was supposed to say were in the jazz funeral scene at the start of the movie when he asks "Where's Strutter?" While originally first in the shooting schedule, that scene was rained off at first attempt.

The boat-chase sequence (shown above), meanwhile, gave Moore his first full injury as Bond. As the boat's engine cut out and it careered into a boathouse, Moore's teeth were damaged and his knee twisted, leaving him walking with a cane for a few days. This is why he's seen sitting in the boat for this scene in the film.

THE 30-SECONDS-A-YEAR SHOT

The Bonfire of the Vanities *1990*

One of the most infamous movie flops of the early 1990s, *The Bonfire of the Vanities* nonetheless contains a notably terrific shot – one that earned its second unit director, Eric Schwab, an extra reward from director Brian De Palma. It's the moment when Concorde lands on the runway at JFK Airport in New York, against the backdrop of the setting sun. Its brilliance lies in the fact that this event happens only once a year and lasts for just 30 seconds.

The two directors had a wager over whether the Concorde landing could be captured for their film. Schwab calculated the exact window of time he'd have to do it, and bet De Palma he could get the shot. It was no small feat, requiring five cameras to record the moment, and it cost De Palma the best part of $100,000 to shoot. Plus, of course, the couple of banknotes he had to hand over to Schwab when the scene did indeed make the final cut.

WHERE'S FACT, WHERE'S FICTION?

Sleepless in Seattle *1993*
You've Got Mail *1998*
Heartburn *1986*

The late Nora Ephron enjoyed many big-screen successes, from her screenplay for *When Harry Met Sally...* (1989) to writing and directing the huge Tom Hanks and Meg Ryan hits *Sleepless in Seattle* and *You've Got Mail*.

Sleepless in Seattle was never intended as a strict remake of 1957's *An Affair to Remember*, as some have suggested, but there's no doubt that the Cary Grant–Deborah Kerr romance greatly influenced Ephron's movie. Not only is *An Affair* referenced in *Sleepless* (indeed, it's the catalyst for Ryan's character making the decisions she does), but it also includes a coming-together at the Empire State Building in New York *and* a Christmas Eve ending.

You've Got Mail actually was a revamp. On release it was billed as a remake of the 1940 movie *The Shop Around the Corner*, but that in itself was based on the 1937 play *Parfumerie* by Miklós László. Ephron references this in the name of the store that Ryan's character owns. She weaves a bit of *Pride and Prejudice* in there too, to the point where Hanks's and Ryan's characters remark on it directly with a chat about Mr Darcy and Miss Bennet. Some have suggested that the movie is a stealth remake of Jane Austen's classic novel, and there are undeniable similarities in the underlying narrative. A bit more emailing in *You've Got Mail*, though.

Ephron (seated on the left in the photo opposite) was well known for allowing her own life into her stories – a fact that makes the 1986 film adaption of her own novel *Heartburn* something of a curio. Although the book was superficially fiction, it was, at heart, the story of Ephron's marriage to Carl Bernstein (also in the photo), which ended in divorce after he had an affair.

This fact had a bearing on the two lead actors, Meryl Streep and Jack Nicholson, when it came to the film, directed by Mike Nichols. Bernstein had secured a legal agreement that he would have the right to see the script in advance and to ensure that his character was played in a sympathetic way. As such, Nichols, an old friend of Bernstein's, reportedly instructed Nicholson that he shouldn't play the part as Carl Bernstein.

This left the actor in the odd position of having to *not* play someone as they really were. Meanwhile, Streep sought to bring as much of the real Ephron as possible to her character. The result is an unusual pair of performances, with one actor striving to be true to the source and the other endeavouring to be anything but. It makes for a fascinating film to watch – if not a very successful one.

THE HAND-CRAFTED FINAL SHOT

Raiders of the Lost Ark *1981*

The final shot of the first Indiana Jones movie, in which the Ark of the Covenant is wheeled into a massive warehouse, is a very funny payoff after we've watched the characters spend so long and suffer so much in searching for it. It's a terrific ending. It's also technically superb, because most of the shot is actually a matte painting. This kind of art is nothing new in movies, of course, but matte paintings were traditionally used for background detail shots. In *Raiders of the Lost Ark*, however, the painting is held in shot for a prolonged period of time. It was created by matte artist Michael Pangrazio and took three months to complete. But the time and effort was worth it. The vast majority of viewers never guessed that every single crate in that shot, apart from the one being wheeled into the warehouse, was hand drawn.

SMALL CLUES

The Terminator *1984*

James Cameron meticulously planned his breakthrough feature film, *The Terminator*, and through the build-up in the movie he proves expert in giving clues as to what's coming. There's a small moment early on, for instance, where Schwarzenegger's Terminator is driving around, looking for the right Sarah Connor. While doing so he rolls over a toy truck, leaving it in pieces. A nod, surely, to the large truck that plays a key role later in the film? Also note the moment when a small dog barks at the Terminator as he walks toward a house. This is echoed later in the movie – while humans struggle to identify Terminators, dogs recognize them straight away. All that metal must have a distinct aroma...

THE JOKE EVERYONE SEEMED TO MISS

The Naked Gun: From the Files of Police Squad! *1988*

There are a few hidden sight jokes and references that, even after umpteen viewings, you may still miss when watching the glorious spoof *The Naked Gun: From the Files of Police Squad!* For example, the scene in which Priscilla Presley's Jane comes tumbling down the stairs isn't just good solid slapstick, the staging is also a tip of the hat to *film noir* classic *Double Indemnity* (1944).

Still, there's one gag in particular that the filmmakers themselves have admitted most people don't get. It comes in the film's opening sequence, and can be spotted on the head of actor David Lloyd Austin who plays Russian leader, Mikhail Gorbachev. Look closely and you'll see that the actor doesn't have an exact replica of Gorbachev's birthmark. Instead, for a joke, the filmmakers shaped it to look like a map of North Vietnam.

YES, CAPTAIN

Halloween *1978*

It's widely known that the original *Halloween* movie was made on a tight budget. As such, some ingenuity was required to bring to the screen exactly what director John Carpenter had in mind. The look of the deadly Michael Myers in the film is a fine example of this. A member of the crew was sent off to buy a cheap mask that could be spray-painted white to give him his sinister look. The mask the crew member returned with was William Shatner in the likeness of Captain Kirk. For a long time even Shatner himself was unaware that one of horror cinema's most infamous pieces of face-wear was actually in his own image.

WATCH CLOSELY!

Get Out *2017*

The character of Rose (Allison Williams) in Jordan Peele's Oscar-winning horror *Get Out* is more nuanced than you might notice at first. Watch again and you'll pick up all sorts of hints about her villainous nature that you may have missed first time around.

One early intervention that Rose makes is during the drive to her parents' house, where she's going to introduce her boyfriend, Chris (Daniel Kaluuya), to her family. When the pair are pulled over by a cop, Rose stands up for Chris, highlighting the officer's apparently racially motivated actions. The cop decides not to take further action, which might seem like a lucky break for the couple, but it's actually bad news for Chris. If they'd been given a ticket, it would have offered a clue for other characters to pick up on later and created a paper trail as evidence for Chris's version of the terrifying events that follow.

Even before then, there's the shocking moment when their car strikes a deer. Look how Chris is hugely concerned, while Rose is completely passive. There's a revealing line right near the start, too, when Rose talks about how she wants to "pry" something out of Chris's dog. Given that we later learn her family are performing brain operations on unwitting victims, it's hard to believe this is an innocent comment. Finally, look out for Rose's hairstyle. Once her dastardly side is exposed, we see her with her hair up – and that's how it stays for the rest of the movie.

THE SMALLER ENDING

Rocky *1976*

I n the original script for *Rocky*, the ending was rather different from the now-iconic finale of the film we all know and love. After Apollo Creed finally defeats Rocky in their world title bout, Rocky was supposed to be carried out on top of the crowd, and in fact this scene was filmed. But the ending didn't click when it was tested and a new one had to be shot. The problem with this was money, which was virtually non-existent. Only a corner of the set could be reconstructed for Rocky's emotional embrace with Adrian – note how close the shots become as the scene develops – and the people filling out the crowd are mostly friends and family, not professional extras. The result was something far more contained, and arguably far more effective.

GRAVITY

Director Alfonso Cuarón worked on *Gravity* for more than five years before it hit the screen in 2013. Starring Sandra Bullock and George Clooney, the film was both a critical and a commercial hit, winning seven Academy Awards, including a Best Director Oscar for Cuarón. It's a film worth taking a closer look at...

1 Alfonso Cuarón is a fan of long shots, without cuts. And you'll see plenty of them in *Gravity*. The opening shot alone runs to over 12 minutes, without a single cut in it! The camera zips around as astronauts seemingly spiral out of control. As you might expect, these shots were technically demanding – ground-breaking even – but they make the movie a real experience, adding to viewers' nausea and discomfort.

2 The space vehicles and the tools that Bullock and Clooney use to repair the space station used time-lapse photographs taken from the real International Space Station for maximum authenticity. The production team had to add signs of wear and tear to them, of course.

3 The voice of mission control, which the two astronauts are in touch with throughout the movie, is that of Oscar-nominated actor Ed Harris.

4 It's estimated that around 80 per cent of what you see on screen in *Gravity* is computer generated to some degree. That's more than, say, James Cameron's far more overtly digital *Avatar* (2009).

5 Cuarón has confirmed that the underlying theme of the film is rebirth. The movie starts with a large bang. Later, we see Bullock's character head into an airlock, where she curls into the fetal position. Her parachute cord symbolises the umbilical cord. When she ultimately lands back on Earth, she pulls herself out of mud and red rocks, effectively becoming reborn on Earth.

6 There's an alternative theory about the film's ending, which suggests that Bullock's character has actually died by the final act. We see her accept death. She turns off her oxygen. She drifts out of consciousness. With lack of oxygen can come hallucinations, including the return of Clooney's character. There's no shortage of white light as her capsule returns to Earth. And when she lands on the surface, her surroundings are idyllic – countryside and birdsong – with nobody else around. Cuarón has denied this interpretation, but it remains an intriguing, if downbeat, idea supported by the on-screen imagery, including the sudden cut to black, as if everything has ended.

ON-SET MOMENTS

One of the rules that many comedy directors abide by is that you can make a film look as improvised and in-the-moment as you like, but if it's not in the script, it rarely works – the written joke almost always outweighs a heavy reliance on ad-libs. There are obvious exceptions, of course. Look at pretty much every speech from Jackie Leason in *Smokey and the Bandit* (1977), for instance, which bore little relation to anything written down. And if you think Steve Carell is in genuine shock and agony getting his chest waxed in *The 40 Year-Old Virgin* (2005), then you'd be correct: that scene was played for real.

What's more, you can have all the planning and storyboarding in the world, but sometimes that little moment of movie magic is something captured in the moment, on the day, whether intended or otherwise.

One famous example concerns the late Heath Ledger in his Oscar-winning turn as the Joker in *The Dark Knight* (2008). In the scene where the character Jim Gordon earns a promotion for capturing him, we suddenly see the Joker giving him an exaggerated round of applause. Was it in the script? No. Was it in the moment – a moment of inspiration from Ledger that he followed through on? Absolutely yes.

Go back further: there's a big crash heard off screen during *It's a Wonderful Life* (1946), as the drunken Uncle Billy staggers away. The crash was actually a member of the crew knocking equipment over. Quick as a flash, Thomas Mitchell's Uncle Billy yells, "I'm alright, I'm alright", turning the accident into a moment that landed in the film.

Throughout this chapter, then, are the tales of tricks, accidents, ideas and guerrilla moments thought up on the spot. They may appear in some cases to have been part of some great plan. But in these instances, they really weren't...

METHOD SMOKING

Easy Rider *1969*

Legend has it that Dennis Hopper's debut behind the camera (which he also starred in), *Easy Rider*, started filming without a completed script in place. This was due to the fact that Hopper and writer/co-star Peter Fonda liked the idea of making it up as they went along, so the movie would come together in-camera. What made this tricky was that, by most accounts, Hopper wasn't the easiest man to work with and was apparently given to screaming at his cast and crew.

He certainly had a lot riding on his directorial debut and he wanted his film to be authentic. As such, when he, Fonda and Jack Nicholson filmed the campfire chat sequence, the three of them... well...they're not *pretending* to smoke marijuana. Between them they inhaled 105 joints before Hopper was satisfied with the scene. Each take required the three men to smoke pretty much a joint to themselves, and the final version that made it into the film took some intensive editing to piece together. It's a particularly testing scene for Nicholson, too. His character starts off speaking normally, but becomes increasingly stoned as the sequence progresses. As the takes mounted up, the challenge was to pretend *not* to be under the influence!

IN NEED OF A HAND

Safety Last! *1923*

The spectacular stunt at the end of *Safety Last!* might well be silent star Harold Lloyd's most iconic moment. We see him hanging precariously from the hands of a clock on top of a skyscraper. While Lloyd wasn't quite as high up as it seems (there's plenty of film trickery at work here), the clock was still positioned on the building nine levels above the ground. And Lloyd really is hanging from it.

What's even more incredible, though, is that he's doing so despite having only one fully usable hand. Several years earlier, Lloyd had lost the thumb, index finger and half the palm of his right hand in an accident with a prop bomb. Throughout subsequent films, including *Safety Last!*, he wore a glove on his right hand which featured prosthetic fingers. If you look closely, you'll see that the thumb on this hand never grabs a rope, clutches onto something or does anything that Lloyd's hardworking left thumb does.

WHAT'S THAT, ORSON?

A Man for All Seasons *1966*

Orson Welles was brought in to co-star in the film adaptation of *A Man for All Seasons*, because the producers were sceptical as to whether Paul Scofield, who had headed the stage production, was a big enough name to headline a movie. In the event, however, Welles wasn't best prepared. Director Fred Zinnemann later revealed that Welles turned up on set without knowing a single line of his dialogue – and that wasn't the only problem. Despite delivering his performance as Cardinal Wolsey in a single day of filming, Welles and Zinnemann didn't see eye to eye, and Welles even claimed that he had Zinnemann removed from the set so he could direct the scenes himself. As it turned out, after the film's release Scofield won huge acclaim and an Oscar for his lead role. Welles was notably absent from any awards list.

THE ARGUMENTS BEHIND A COMEDY CLASSIC

Tootsie *1982*

There's a school of thought that says if you have a calm movie set, you get a poor movie. It's easy to debunk this theory (take a look at the wonderful 2014 movie *Pride*, where the writer and director unusually sat side by side throughout production); however, the idea also suggests that if you have a troubled set the sparks make for a better film – and it's hard to argue against that in the case of classic comedy *Tootsie*.

Star Dustin Hoffman and director Sydney Pollack were at loggerheads for the bulk of the production, and arguments were widely reported even at the point of the film's release. Despite this (or perhaps because of it) it was Hoffman who came up with the idea of Pollack taking on the role of his agent in the movie. The blunt scenes between the two characters reflected the tensions that were bubbling behind the scenes. The pair never made a film together again.

You might also notice that Bill Murray's name is missing from the opening credits of the film. This was deliberate for two reasons. Filmmakers wanted Murray's appearance to be a surprise for audiences, but they also aimed to avoid expectations that the film would be a Bill Murray-esque comedy. Despite his absence from the opening credits, though, Murray undeniably had an impact on the way the film developed. His dialogue is pretty much entirely improvised. And the reason the apartment he shares with Hoffman's character is so messy is because on his first day of filming, he went through the set and basically trashed it. His logic? He figured the characters would live in a mess!

KEEP YOUR

HAIR OFF

Superman *1978*
Alien 3 *1992*
Fear and Loathing in Las Vegas *1998*
Fahrenheit 451 *1966*

An early piece of promotional material for *Superman* shows Gene Hackman as Lex Luthor – with a moustache. Yes, the famously smooth-skinned villain is sporting facial hair. Since his Oscar-winning performance in *The French Connection* (1971), Hackman had been enjoying no shortage of star power, and the story goes that when *Superman* director Richard Donner asked him to shave off his moustache for the role of Luthor, Hackman refused. In the film itself, however, you'll see that the moustache has gone. That's down to a bit of sneakiness from

Donner, who told Hackman that he'd shave his own facial hair if the actor did the same. After Hackman had duly shaved off his moustache, Donner promptly ripped off his own, revealing that he'd been wearing a fake all along!

Alien 3 marked the feature directorial debut of acclaimed helmer David Fincher. Fincher wanted the character of Ellen Ripley, played by Sigourney Weaver, to be bald, and Weaver gamely shaved her head for the role throughout the initial shoot. But when it came to the later

reshoots, she preferred not to chop her mop again, and opted for a skullcap instead. See if you can work out which bits are which.

Tobey Maguire also proved reluctant to shave his hair again when the time for reshoots on *Fear and Loathing in Las Vegas* came around. He reportedly asked for an extra fee to do so, which the studio refused. Instead, he was given a head cap – and a rather unconvincing one at that. It took some digital effects work to make Maguire's fake baldness look real.

One person who messed with their hair on purpose was actor Oskar Werner, who played the role of Guy Montag in François Truffaut's adaptation of Ray Bradbury's *Fahrenheit 451*. There had been disagreements between both actor and director throughout shooting, and a consequence of this can be spotted at the end of the film. There's a scene where Werner's hair is noticeably shorter than anywhere else in the movie – apparently a statement of protest by the actor, who did it deliberately to create a continuity problem.

CHILLED TO THE BONES

Poltergeist *1982*

S everal stories surrounding the huge horror hit *Poltergeist* have emerged since its release, not least how involved Steven Spielberg was in directing the film (it proved a point of debate for some time whether Spielberg or Tobe Hooper actually directed the final cut). But one of the most bone-chilling tales about the making of this movie relates to the swimming-pool scene, in which JoBeth Williams's character flees from the house and lands in the backyard swimming pool, which is filled with skeletons. If you think the look on her face is genuine fear, you'd be right. The skeletons were, in fact, real. Williams had been given this information in advance, which had only worsened her fear and made her increasingly reluctant to shoot the scene. She got through the shooting, but wasn't very happy about it…

SURPRISE!

Die Hard *1988*

Few actors fall from a great height as convincingly as the late Alan Rickman at the end of the 1980s classic *Die Hard*. In the scene, Rickman's villainous Hans Gruber plunges to his death. In real life, of course, Rickman was falling from a much lower height onto a safe landing pad. The stunt team told Rickman they'd drop him on the count of three, but in the event they pulled the rug on him, letting him go on the count of one. The surprise on his face as his character is falling is entirely genuine. No wonder it's so convincing...

DANCING THROUGH THE AIR

Royal Wedding *1951*

One of Fred Astaire's most legendary dance sequences is the "ceiling" number from *Royal Wedding*. It lasts nearly four minutes without a single cut, and sees Astaire dancing up the walls, on the ceiling, back down the walls then on the floor again. What's really incredible is that he's effectively doing it all for real. The whole room in this scene was constructed inside a metal gimbal, which rotated as Astaire danced. So, on top of the usual extensive choreography the actor had to keep track of, he had to know where the room was going to be, too! It was a perilous number to perform, and risked serious injury, so there was no margin for error. He danced against gravity, and nobody noticed a thing. Incredible.

THAT'S OUT OF ORDER

Brief Encounter *1945*

I t's not often that a film is shot entirely in sequence, but sometimes mixing things up is a deliberate creative decision. That was certainly the case with *Brief Encounter*, as David Lean's film about two strangers meeting in a railway station was designed to leave the audience feeling as conflicted as the two main characters. After all, if the romance developed, Celia Johnson's character would be cheating on her husband – and this was the 1940s! Lean didn't want Johnson and co-star Trevor Howard to feel settled, preferring to try to put them through the emotional turbulence their characters would be experiencing. As such, the schedule was put together in a way that purposely mixed up the chronology of the story. It's fair to say it had the desired effect.

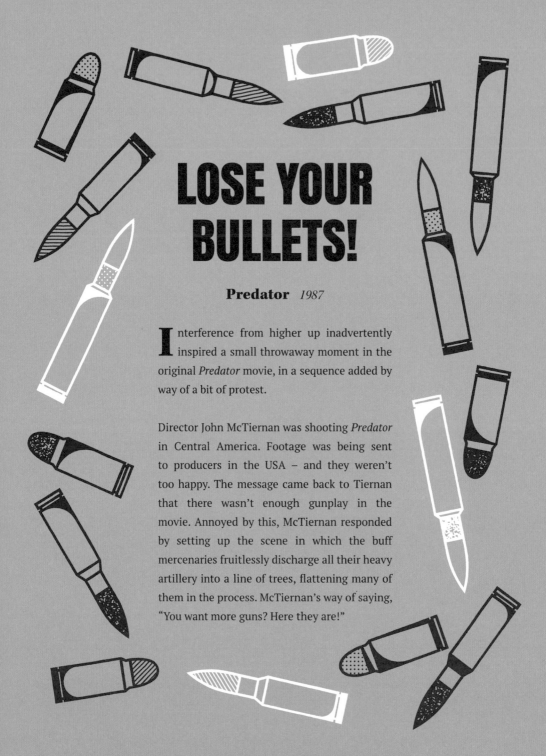

LOSE YOUR BULLETS!

Predator *1987*

Interference from higher up inadvertently inspired a small throwaway moment in the original *Predator* movie, in a sequence added by way of a bit of protest.

Director John McTiernan was shooting *Predator* in Central America. Footage was being sent to producers in the USA – and they weren't too happy. The message came back to Tiernan that there wasn't enough gunplay in the movie. Annoyed by this, McTiernan responded by setting up the scene in which the buff mercenaries fruitlessly discharge all their heavy artillery into a line of trees, flattening many of them in the process. McTiernan's way of saying, "You want more guns? Here they are!"

MIRROR IMAGE

Sunset Boulevard *1950*
Black Swan *2010*
Taxi Driver *1976*

In a striking underwater shot (shown above) at the start of *Sunset Boulevard*, we see the body of screenwriter Joe Gillis (played by William Holden) face down in a swimming pool, his eyes wide open. Nothing too unusual there, you might think – this is classic *film noir* after all – but what's noteworthy about this scene is that it was achieved by filming from *above* the pool.

Director Billy Wilder wanted the shot to show an underwater perspective, as if seen by a fish swimming in the pool. But there were no underwater cameras in 1950, so a certain amount of ingenuity was required. What you actually see is a reflection. The filmmakers dropped the water temperature to below 9°C (48°F) to ensure there was no distortion, then they placed a mirror at the bottom of the pool. They positioned the camera at the edge of the pool and, by framing the mirror below the surface, the effect of an underwater shot was achieved.

Mirrors are often used for more upfront storytelling, too. *Black Swan* is awash with shots of mirrors, as Natalie Portman's Nina is constantly presented with an image of herself as her mind starts to internally fracture. Watch how many times the film actively forces her to simply look at herself.

Then there's one of the most famous mirror scenes of all time, when Robert De Niro's Travis Bickle stares himself down in *Taxi Driver*. His "you talkin' to me?" monologue was only partly in the script. Paul Schrader had penned that Bickle would practise his quick-draw technique in front of the mirror, but it was De Niro who added one of cinema's most-quoted lines.

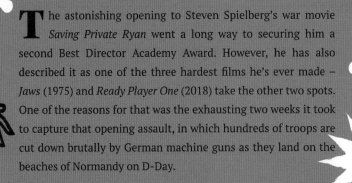

WHAT THE ACTORS COULDN'T SEE

Saving Private Ryan *1998*

The astonishing opening to Steven Spielberg's war movie *Saving Private Ryan* went a long way to securing him a second Best Director Academy Award. However, he has also described it as one of the three hardest films he's ever made – *Jaws* (1975) and *Ready Player One* (2018) take the other two spots. One of the reasons for that was the exhausting two weeks it took to capture that opening assault, in which hundreds of troops are cut down brutally by German machine guns as they land on the beaches of Normandy on D-Day.

Andrew Scott – who has subsequently found fame in the TV show *Sherlock* and films such as *Pride* (2014) – was one of the extras filming on Curracloe Beach in Ireland, which stood in for the Normandy landing grounds. He recalled that they couldn't even see the camera because the beach was awash with smoke. Every actor was given a specific path to follow, but the dirt flying from various effects was real and it was often impossible to see where they were going. The squibs, loud explosions and fake limbs you see in that opening scene led to actors often struggling to find exactly where they were supposed to be going in all the mayhem.

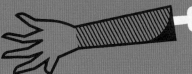

IS THAT YOU, CAPTAIN?

Frankie and Johnny *1991*

The remake of the stage play *Frankie and Johnny* attracted some early controversy when Kathy Bates – who had won acclaim for the role on stage – was replaced with the Hollywood glamour of Michelle Pfeiffer for the movie. Less controversial was the choice of Al Pacino to play opposite her, and one on-set anecdote from the shooting of this film concerns a joke played on the iconic actor.

There's a scene in which Pacino opens the door to his apartment and a look of startled surprise crosses his face. This is entirely genuine. Unbeknownst to Pacino, *Star Trek VI: The Undiscovered Country* (1991) was shooting on a nearby soundstage. *Frankie and Johnny* director Garry Marshall arranged for its stars DeForest Kelley, William Shatner and Leonard Nimoy (pictured left, front row, second from left to right) to be waiting behind the door. You don't see them on screen, but you do see Pacino's reaction!

JULIE VS. THE HELICOPTER

The Sound of Music *1965*

One of the most iconic opening scenes in cinema sees Julie Andrews running through the ostensibly Austrian (actually Bavarian) mountains, belting out the title song to *The Sound of Music*. Her beaming smile belies the fact that this wasn't the easiest scene to film. Besides the fact that there's a member of the crew squirrelled away in the bushes, giving Andrews her cue through a megaphone, there's also the fact that the scene was shot from a helicopter. Andrews had to appear to run effortlessly through the balmy air when she could barely stand upright against the wind the helicopter was generating. And she had to sing against the force of it, too. Unsurprisingly, this shot required a lot of takes to get in the can...

THE ILLUSION IN A MOVIE ENDING

Field of Dreams *1989*

The denouement to *Field of Dreams* gives the impression that what you're seeing is a large number of cars snaking their way to a small corner of Iowa. It's worth taking another look at that shot, though, to see some movie-illusion magic at work.

The cars were all lined up for real, with director Phil Alden Robinson and his team transmitting instructions to the drivers using local radio. The shot itself took three attempts to get in the can, but in fact only the cars at the front are moving. Look back along the line and you'll see that every other vehicle is still. To simulate movement, drivers in the other cars were told to blink their headlights. It was a surprisingly effective way to fake a motor pilgrimage to a baseball field in corn country.

PLANE STUNTS
FOR REAL

Hell's Angels *1930*
Tora! Tora! Tora! *1970*

Howard Hughes's love of film and aviation were explored in Martin Scorsese's movie *The Aviator* (2004). Like Scorsese, Hughes was an innovator when it came to his movies. *Hell's Angels* (shown opposite) started out as a silent picture, but after the release of the first "talkie" – *The Jazz Singer* (1927) – Hughes adapted his film to accommodate spoken dialogue.

The film earned notoriety for its final sequence – still regarded as one of the most dangerous ever to make it to the final cut of a movie. The aerial dogfight sequences throughout were shot with the help of pilots who had flown in World War I. In all, 137 pilots were employed to realize the final scenes, and three people were killed during the filming of the aerial shots in the movie.

There's a moment toward the end where, after a strafing mission, a plane has to pull out steeply. It was considered so dangerous that the only person willing to do the stunt was Howard

Hughes himself. The warnings of danger proved right. Hughes crashed the plane, and fractured his skull, requiring surgery on his face. He did get his shot, though. You can experience a flavour of just what was involved in the making of *Hell's Angels* by watching the opening part of Scorsese's *The Aviator*.

A perilous shot of a stunt going wrong is also included in *Tora! Tora! Tora!* A retelling of the attack on Pearl Harbor in 1941, during World War II (and a co-production between Japanese and American filmmakers), the movie has some notable plane sequences, one of which involves an aircraft careering across an airfield, smashing into planes and heading toward fleeing extras. Thing is, the extras are fleeing for real. The plane was a prop, which was in theory being guided via remote control. But the controls went wrong and the plane went off-course. The camera kept rolling, nobody got hurt, and the sequence made it to the film.

CHANGE OF CHARACTER

The Great Escape *1963*

Steve McQueen wasn't a happy man on the set of the war movie classic *The Great Escape*. But in fact it was his discontent that sparked what has arguably become the most famous sequence in the film.

The problems began when McQueen expressed his disappointment with the rough cut of the first six weeks of shooting. The day after watching the footage, he didn't turn up on set, instead demanding that his part in the film – the character of Virgil Hilts ("The Cooler King") – be rewritten. This was a tall order so late in the day, but McQueen and co-stars James Garner (whom at one point McQueen accused of trying to make the film his own) and James Coburn cooked up a plan that resulted in a change to the movie, and most notably a change to McQueen's character within it. Through this, he became more of an independent force, which is why in the final film you see him always trying to escape by himself and become increasingly separate from the main group.

Furthermore, the reason you see McQueen's character playing with a baseball mitt and glove throughout the film (and at the end of the film, too) was to pacify the actor.

Then there's the motorcycle escape sequence. Hilts gets the bike by stringing a wire across a road, where a German biker hits it. If you're quick enough, you might just spot that the actor playing the German motorcyclist is... Steve McQueen. For the key stunt, though – the legendary jump across the border fence – McQueen deferred to a stuntman. Legend says that McQueen, a keen motorcyclist, first attempted the jump himself but failed to pull it off. Bud Ekins stepped in and completed the sequence. McQueen was always careful to give him the credit, too.

THE COSTUME

Batman *1989*

Like any actor who plays the superhero, Michael Keaton takes on two roles in Tim Burton's ground-breaking 1989 comic-book movie, *Batman*. One way he differentiates them physically is by the slow, deliberate way that he turns when facing foes in the guise of Batman. Where the character of Bruce Wayne turns his neck, note how Batman moves his whole body. In fact, this was less a character choice than a clothing restriction. When Keaton originally tried to move his neck too much in his Batman costume, he ripped the suit and this is what led him to change the way Batman moved on screen.

SCENES SHOT ON THE QUIET

Forrest Gump *1994*
The Bourne Identity *2002*
Two Mules for Sister Sara *1970*

orrest Gump's marathon run across America is one of the key ingredients in the hugely successful Oscar-winning movie of the same name. Capturing the run would require filming on location at various sites across the United States. But at an estimated $1.6 million even to film these scenes with a skeleton crew and no extra days in the schedule, this was going to take up far too much of the movie's $46 million budget. Star Tom Hanks and director Robert Zemeckis put their heads together and came up with a drastic solution to the problem. Basically, they'd stump up $800,000 apiece of their own money. Zemeckis,

Hanks and as small a team as they could get away with, headed off around the country at weekends. That's why those moments made it into the movie: had they not paid for them themselves, it's likely they wouldn't have been shot at all.

But at least the studio knew. In the case of *The Bourne Identity*, director Doug Liman had a frosty relationship with Universal Studios (one reason why he departed the franchise after just one movie), and had regular battles with them throughout production. At the end of shooting, there was a short confrontation scene in particular featuring Matt Damon's Bourne and Clive Owen's assassin, The Professor, which took place in the Czech Republic. Liman felt that what he'd shot wasn't quite working, and asked for permission to fine-tune it with a little extra material. He wanted another run at it the following morning, before they flew back to Los Angeles. The studio refused. As a result, Liman decided to go behind their back and get his new shots anyway, without asking permission. They're all in the movie.

Even legendary director Don Siegel did that once. He was shooting *Two Mules for Sister Sara*, starring Clint Eastwood (their second collaboration), and a sizeable problem presented itself. Shirley MacLaine, who played Sister Sara in the film, couldn't ride a mule. The script mandated that she needed to for pretty much the entire film. Plus there was the small matter that the film's title implied it too.

Siegel got Eastwood and MacLaine together, and tried to come up with a solution that wouldn't require going back to Universal – the studio backing the film – for permission. MacLaine felt she could tackle riding a smaller burro, and thus the trio came up with a new scene that they wrote between them and shot. When you see Sara trade the mule she originally has (see below, left) for a burro (see below, right) in the movie, that was all done behind the studio's back. As Siegel noted in his memoir, the studio executives didn't even notice the change.

REFERENCING OLD FRIENDS

Goodfellas *1990*

Comfortably one of the most iconic and memorable scenes of Martin Scorsese's gangster classic *Goodfellas* is the moment when Joe Pesci's Tommy – on Oscar-winning form – takes Ray Liotta's Henry Hill to task for calling him "funny". The "funny how?" sequence that follows is a masterclass in building and releasing tension.

Incredibly, though, the scene wasn't scripted. In fact, it harks back to an experience Joe Pesci had when he was younger, where he did indeed tell a gangster in the restaurant he worked at that he thought he was funny. Pesci told Scorsese this story, and the director thought there was something in it but he wanted it to feel spur-of-the-moment. He therefore included it in the film but didn't script it. The surprised reactions from the supporting cast in the scene are very much the real thing – they didn't know the dialogue was coming.

WARGAMES

Bringing the story of *WarGames*, starring Matthew Broderick, to the screen in 1983 was an exhausting venture for director John Badham. He needed a visually impressive set for the key NORAD headquarters, to get across the cinema of a room where nuclear war could be instigated at the touch of a button. He and his team came up with something special.

1 The set for *WarGames* was, at the time, the most expensive ever built. Estimates put the construction of the set alone for the film at around $1 million. This was at a time when a mid-range movie was costing $10–15 million for the final production, pre-marketing and distribution expenses.

2 While preparing the set, the design team wasn't allowed to see the actual NORAD facility that they were basing their ideas on, so they let loose with their imaginations. After filming had wrapped, they got to see the real-life equivalent and discovered it was a lot more basic and boring than the version they'd created. Legend goes that eventually, the real NORAD command centre was remodelled to look more like the movie guestimate.

3 The huge screens on the walls are all driven by massive projectors, which had to be perfectly synced, otherwise the scenes taking place in front of them simply wouldn't work. Five screens were used in all, and that meant that the displays were working on-set (rather than requiring post-production trickery) for the actors to react against.

4 The reason the production required this projection technology was that the computers used in *WarGames* – while costing tens of thousands of dollars – were unable to output the graphics to a screen that size! But then, this was the early 1980s...

5 In all, some 84 war computer screens are in view on the NORAD set, and getting them synced up was one of the most exhausting visual effects challenges of the movie.

6 The film must have been convincing. Just over a year later, the then-US president Ronald Reagan signed the National Policy on Telecommunications and Automated Information Systems Security. Reagan had seen a screening of *WarGames*, and was vexed and concerned by whether it could come true. He thus started a series of conversations that would eventually lead to the new policy.

INSPIRATIONS AND RAMIFICATIONS

When Steven Spielberg's *Jaws* was released in 1975, it changed the public's perception of the humble shark. Although few people were likely to consider them as pet material before that, one ramification of Spielberg's intense, skilful first blockbuster was that sharks were suddenly brought into the spotlight as killing machines. The fear of these fish that the film sparked continues to this day, despite the best efforts of educators to dispel the myth of murderous great whites. And of course *Jaws* had ramifications within the film industry, too, proving an inspiration for many subsequent movies. *The Meg* (2018), *Deep Blue Sea* (1999), *47 Meters Down* (2017) and many others pay tribute to the movie that carved open this particular cinematic and aquatic niche. Because if you're making a shark movie now, how can you not talk about it?

The most obvious reaction to a hit film, after all, is that people go away and try to mimic it...and cash in. When first *Porky's* (1981) and then *American Pie* (1999) hit big for two different generations, a couple of decades apart, each ignited a fresh wave of cheap, gross-out comedies. The stunning success of the *Paranormal Activity* and *Saw* films in their own way ignited a wave of ultra-low budget imitators, and it was the massive profits that the *Saw* sequels generated that, for instance, afforded Lionsgate the funds and clout to bring *The Hunger Games* series to the screen.

Conversely, in a story often told, the huge cost overruns of Michael Cimino's *Heaven's Gate* (1980), a film whose lavish taste is clear as day on screen, would lead to the collapse of the long-running United Artists studio as it was in its then form. (It's now a label for another company, rather than a studio in its own right.)

But box office business aside, films can have a much more notable impact beyond the silver screen. In extreme cases, laws can be changed. Sometimes rules are altered, copyrights dismissed, or the path of cinema itself diverted just a little as a result of them.

These are the examples we explore in this chapter – the inspirations and ramifications of films that have influenced other movies or even changed the world in some small way. And not always for the better...

INELIGIBLE

Aladdin *1992*

The late Robin Williams extensively ad-libbed in his role as the Genie in Disney's animated hit *Aladdin*, reportedly recording around 16 hours of material in the end. For instance, the opening scene of the movie, where a street merchant introduces the film, was made up on the spot by the actor, as he reacted to objects that were placed on a table in front of him on the recording sound stage.

Disney had high hopes of Oscar glory for *Aladdin*, especially after *Beauty and the Beast* (1991) had broken a ceiling by becoming the first animated feature to garner a Best Picture Academy Award nomination. But no such honours were to come *Aladdin's* way. A campaign to get Williams a Best Actor nomination came to nothing, and Disney's attempt to earn a Best Adapted Screenplay prize was dismissed before it even got going. The problem? All that ad-libbing! The extent to which Williams had strayed from the scripted word fell foul of the Academy's eligibility requirements, which required far more of the written screenplay to be delivered.

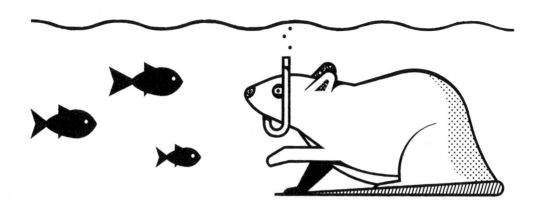

THE EXTENDED CUT BY ACCIDENT

The Abyss *1989*

Today, cuts of James Cameron's *The Abyss* – a film that broke down visual effects doors and paved the way for *Terminator 2: Judgment Day* (1991) a few years later – now include as standard a shot that caused some consternation at the time of the movie's original release. In fact, it was excised altogether from the British theatrical cut of the film, and only came to public light due to a mix-up at a British television company.

The moment in question is the one demonstrating "fluid breathing", showing that rats can breathe with their lungs full of liquid. This is a real thing, too, with a scientific backbone to it. In the original UK cinema release of *The Abyss*, there was a quick cutaway to hide the fact that the rats in question (and

they were real – five rats were used for five takes) soiled themselves when they started breathing in liquid. Even though they were ultimately unharmed, as Cameron noted, "the Royal Veterinarian felt that it was painful for the rat", so the key shots were removed.

However, when the film got its television premiere in Britain, the broadcaster Channel 4 accidentally showed the wrong version. As such, the sequence with close-up shots of a rat breathing liquid was screened for the first time in the UK, even though the British Board of Film Classification (BBFC) hadn't approved it. Channel 4 earned a fine for its mistake, but as a consequence the full version became widely available and the scene that caused so much trouble can now be seen in every cut.

PUBLIC DOMAIN

Saving Happy Birthday *2016*
10 *1979*

If you've ever wondered why you never hear the song "Happy Birthday to You" at a seemingly appropriate moment in a low-budget production, chances are it was to do with the licensing. A documentary project from filmmaker Jennifer Nelson proved an unlikely catalyst in changing all that, in one of history's more contentious music copyright cases.

For decades, it was believed that the traditional song was under the ownership of the company Warner/Chappell Music, Inc., which was merrily pocketing a licence fee every time "Happy Birthday" was used. Nelson was working on a documentary about the 100th anniversary of the song, and was set to be charged $1,500 for the rights to use it herself. She brought a court case to challenge Warner/Chappell's rights (which she documented in her film, *Saving Happy Birthday*) – and won. As a consequence, the song has been released into the public domain, more than a century after it was composed.

Ravel's classic *Boléro* nearly ended up taking longer than usual to reach the public domain,

a situation that was due in no small part to the comedy *10*, starring Dudley Moore and Bo Derek. In the film, Moore's and Derek's characters participate in some...well...let's call it "duvet dancing", while *Boléro* plays in the background. This sparked a fresh wave of interest in the music as people decided to try it out for themselves! As they flocked to buy the piece, royalty earnings went through the roof. The fact that British ice-skaters Torvill and Dean won gold at the 1984 Winter Olympics with a dramatic routine set to the piece also contributed to its massive success. By the end of the 1980s, *Boléro* was allegedly earning over a million dollars a year in licensing fees for Ravel's estate.

This all came to an end in May 2016, when the copyright lapsed and the piece entered the public domain in many countries. But *Boléro* had become so lucrative that Ravel's estate brought a court case to extend the copyright. The action proved unsuccessful, but you can understand why the estate was so reluctant to give up its golden goose.

A SILVER LINING

The Day After Tomorrow *2004*

Director Roland Emmerich's climate-change disaster movie *The Day After Tomorrow* was loudly scoffed at by critics, despite the sizeable haul of cash it took at the box office. But shortly after its release, research from Yale University suggested that the movie had had quite an impact on audiences. The Yale research concluded that "the movie appears to have had a strong influence on watchers' risk perceptions of global warming", further claiming that it "had a significant impact on the climate change risk perceptions, conceptual models, behavioral intentions, policy priorities, and even voting intentions of moviegoers". Who'd have thought it?

THE PRESIDENT IS NOT AMUSED

Contact *1997*

The footage you see of Bill Clinton in the sci-fi hit *Contact* actually caused some discontent at the White House. Director Robert Zemeckis uses parts of several news conferences that Clinton gave during his tenure as president, but one in particular ruffled the administration's feathers. This was a briefing Clinton had given in 1996, discussing a rock that was believed to have originated on the planet Mars.

In the movie, Clinton is heard to say, "If this discovery is confirmed, it will surely be one of the most stunning insights into our universe that science has ever uncovered. Its implications are as far-reaching and awe-inspiring as can be imagined." Those lines weren't scripted; they were the real words Clinton spoke at the conference. The problem was that the filmmakers, who edited the cast of the film into the scene, hadn't specifically sought White House permission to use the footage in such a way. Moreover, Clinton himself was unaware that he would be appearing in the film until it was finished.

In an unusual action where films are concerned, the White House issued a formal complaint to Warner Bros., formalizing the administration's displeasure at the way separate footage had been edited into the movie. Still, they didn't request that the sequence was removed, and it remains in the final cut of the feature.

Hollywood productions haven't repeated the trick since – at least, not in a fictional context. Spike Lee edited footage of Donald Trump into 2018's *BlacKkKlansman*, but no attempt was made to fictionalize his words.

I NOW PRONOUNCE YOU...

Bram Stoker's Dracula *1992*

A desire for utter authenticity is the driving force for some moviemakers, and none more so than the multiple Oscar-winning director Francis Ford Coppola. For example, when filming *Bram Stoker's Dracula*, he wasn't happy with early takes of the marriage ceremony between the characters of Jonathan and Elisabeta, played by Keanu Reeves and Winona Ryder, so he decided to try the scene with a real priest in a real Greek Orthodox church, shooting the entire ceremony from start to finish. Some 25 years later it came to light that Coppola's desire for realism may have resulted in Reeves and Ryder being married for real in the scene. When asked about it, Coppola agreed that the wedding ceremony may indeed have been legally binding.

OH LORD

Chariots of Fire *1981*

The Oscar-winning *Chariots of Fire* features a scene where Harold Abrahams becomes the first person to successfully complete what's known as the "Great Court Run". This is a Cambridge University challenge, in which students try to run the length of Trinity College's Great Court perimeter in the time it takes the college clock to strike noon.

What you see in the film, though, is deliberate historical inaccuracy, introduced as a consequence of a permission disagreement. Abrahams never even attempted the run; it was actually a student called Lord David Burghley who first completed the challenge in 1927 – a young man who went on to become a Conservative politician in the UK. The story goes that when it came to the film, producer David Puttnam gave the achievement to Abrahams because he wasn't a fan of Burghley's politics. In retaliation, Burghley – then in his seventies – withdrew permission for his name to be used in the movie. As a result, the character that effectively represents him is known as Lord Andrew Lindsay in the film.

IN TIME TO THE MUSIC

Close Encounters of the Third Kind *1977*
Baby Driver *2017*

U sually, a movie's musical score is one of the last things to be completed. For *Close Encounters of the Third Kind*, however, director Steven Spielberg and composer John Williams inverted that. It's a movie that's very tightly edited around Williams's score, and Spielberg was able to do that because he already had the music to work to in advance of shooting. Spielberg and Williams have worked on many, many films since, but following the more common practice of the composer working from footage of the film.

Edgar Wright went a step further with his 2017 hit *Baby Driver*. The director knew the music he wanted for his movie before production began, which meant that he could direct the actor's movements to match the beats of the soundtrack. In fact, individual edits and acting beats are constantly in time to the heartbeat of the musical tracks that Wright chose, and intricately choreographed for his film.

An aside on *Baby Driver*. The reason that masks of the actor Mike Myers are used in the film is because producers couldn't get permission to use masks of the infamous killer Michael Myers, of the *Halloween* films – which were the same masks that were based on William Shatner (see "Yes, Captain", page 77). If *Baby Driver* had been given permission to use them, what you would have seen was a mask of a man in a mask!

GET ME MORE SCRAT

Ice Age *2002–16*

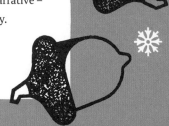

A cross the *Ice Age* franchise of animated movies, the most popular character is a squirrel called Scrat, whose quest for an acorn remains the highlight of the series. Yet his first appearance, in the opening scene of the first *Ice Age* film (2002), was also supposed to be his last – at the close of the sequence, Scrat ends up on the bottom of a large, unidentified creature's foot, and is marched off to his fate. But when the scene was used in the first trailer for the movie, Scrat was an instant hit. When the film got as far as test screenings without him appearing in any other scene, audiences demanded to know where Scrat was. As a result of the character's popularity, the studio, Blue Sky, quickly went back and gave him a bigger role. That's why Scrat's appearances don't really knit to the story, and have a feel of sketches to break up the movie's main narrative – they were added relatively late in the day.

ARNIE'S UNLIKELY INSPIRATION

Red Heat *1988*
Ninotchka *1939*

The first time that Arnold Schwarzenegger was asked to contain his action-man persona in a US film was probably *Red Heat*, in which he played a stern Russian officer alongside James Belushi's less conventional American cop. If you've ever wondered who Schwarzenegger channelled to get into the role, he revealed the answer in his memoir.

Apparently, he was asked by director Walter Hill to watch the work of Greta Garbo, in particular her 1939 movie *Ninotchka*. It was from viewing that movie that Schwarzenegger worked out how a loyal Soviet Union officer should behave in the western world. He reckons he clicked as to what his performance should be as a result of that direction.

OPPORTUNE CASTING

Mission: Impossible – Fallout *2018*
Slaughterhouse Rulez *2018*
Eyes Wide Shut *1999*
Mission: Impossible II *2000*

X-Men *2000*
The Greatest Showman *2017*

Sometimes, something happens on one film that has an unanticipated effect on another. For example, when filming of *Mission: Impossible – Fallout* was shut down in 2017 to allow leading man Tom Cruise to recover from a broken ankle (see "More Pain", page 52), *Fallout* co-star Simon Pegg found he had some extra time on his hands. As a result, his role in another project, *Slaughterhouse Rulez* (on which he was also one of the producers), was beefed up to take advantage of his unexpected availability.

But this isn't the only *Mission: Impossible* delay that's had a casting knock-on. Had Stanley Kubrick not spent around two years filming his final movie, *Eyes Wide Shut*, Tom Cruise would have been free to make *Mission: Impossible II*

sooner. If that had happened then that film's starring villain, Dougray Scott, would have completed the project in time to take on the role of Wolverine in the first *X-Men* movie as planned. Unfortunately for Scott, the significant delays meant he had to forego *X-Men*, leaving a then-unknown actor named Hugh Jackman to take the role.

Talking of Jackman, if you watch the credits of his musical hit *The Greatest Showman* carefully, you might just be able to make out a tip of the hat to Wolverine. *Logan* (2017) director James Mangold helped out in post-production on *The Greatest Showman*, and when his name comes up in the credits, in the corner of the screen is a pattern in which the claws are very much out...

THE COEN BROTHERS' WAY

Blood Simple *1984*
True Romance *1993*

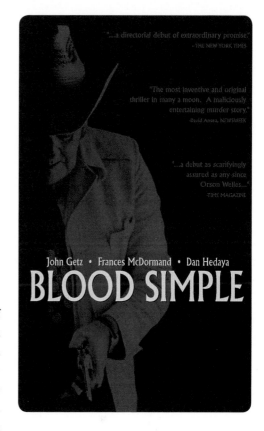

"...a directorial debut of extraordinary promise."
– THE NEW YORK TIMES

"The most inventive and original thriller in many a moon. A maliciously entertaining murder story."
–David Ansen, NEWSWEEK

"...a debut as scarifyingly assured as any since Orson Welles..."
TIME MAGAZINE

John Getz • Frances McDormand • Dan Hedaya
BLOOD SIMPLE

Joel and Ethan Coen burst to prominence off the back of their debut *Blood Simple*, a lean and highly regarded thriller made on a very slim budget (and one of the few films with a later-released Director's Cut that's shorter than the original theatrical release). The film was written with two things in mind – the project's tight purse strings and the Coens' determination to make their name with this movie.

Among those inspired by this path was Quentin Tarantino. When Tarantino wrote *True Romance*, he did so thinking that he would direct the movie himself, and he followed a similar economic approach to that used by the Coens in order to make it happen. In Tarantino's case, Terrence Malick's *Badlands* (1973) would be a notable influence on the movie, not least in Hans Zimmer's familiar score.

Eventually, Tarantino gave his blessing for Tony Scott to direct *True Romance* rather than tackling it himself, opting to make his own cinematic feature directing debut with *Reservoir Dogs* in 1992 instead (which ended up actually filming before *True Romance*). But signing over the project to another filmmaker ultimately led to a change in the structure of the film. Tarantino's original screenplay (which was later published) told the story out of order – the same approach that he took with *Pulp Fiction* (1994) – but the finished movie took a much more typical, chronological path. Tony Scott did reportedly try to cut a version of the film that ordered scenes as per Tarantino's original, but soon abandoned the idea, believing the chronological approach was the right way to go.

THE FILM WITH THE COPYRIGHTED TATTOO

The Hangover Part II *2011*

The hugely successful follow-up to *The Hangover* (2009) may have basically repeated the story of the first film. Yet one of the new additions to *The Hangover Part II* led to its very release being thrown into jeopardy. And a simple tattoo was at the heart of the problem.

In the film, the character of Stu (played by Ed Helms, below) awakens after a very heavy night with a tattoo on his face – a replica of the tribal face inking sported by Mike Tyson (below right)

who cameoed in the film. It was designed by S Victor Whitmill specifically for Tyson. Not, Whitmill insisted, for Helms. The artist was so unhappy that the tattoo had been copied that he launched a lawsuit against Warner Bros., claiming that his design was copyrighted and had been used without permission. The proceedings looked set to delay the release of the film so Warner Bros. blinked first and paid Whitmill in an out-of-court settlement. Thus, the tattoo joke proved to be the most expensive one in the film.

THE GROUND-BREAKING USE OF TECHNOLOGY

Bound for Glory *1976*

I t may not be as high profile as some of director Hal Ashby's other films, such as *Shampoo* (1975) and *Being There* (1979), but *Bound for Glory* is nonetheless an interesting feature – and a quietly ground-breaking one. Its claim to fame? In the scene that takes viewers through a migrant camp, what you're witnessing is the first use of a Steadicam in a feature film. Now a taken-for-granted part of the filmmaking arsenal, the technology was created by inventor Garrett Brown. But of real note in *Bound for Glory* is that the shot in question starts from a particularly high level, which meant that Brown had to start on the crane rig himself, before setting off with the camera and following around the actor playing Woody Guthrie, David Carradine. The film would ultimately take home Oscar gold for its cinematography.

ADMIN ERROR

Night of the Living Dead *1968*

George A Romero's low-budget zombie movie *Night of the Living Dead* was a hit on release, and over time has proved to be a hugely influential horror flick. But one of the reasons for its initial popularity may have been an administration error.

During production, the film went by the working title *Night of the Flesh Eaters*, but just before its release the decision was made to change it. The distributors duly slotted in a title card announcing that this was *Night of the Living Dead*, but what they failed to do was include a copyright notice. This turned out to be a costly oversight. It wasn't until 1976 that an act of law protected motion pictures whether or not they had a copyright notice on screen; before that, any movie without one was considered copyright-free. Which meant that *Night of the Living Dead* went straight into the public domain – anyone was allowed to screen or publish a copy of the film.

That missing notice affected how the sequels divvied up, too. Romero and co-writer John Russo both wanted to turn the movie into a series, but disagreed about the direction it should take. As neither of them could claim greater rights to the film than the other, they came up with a deal. Romero's sequels (which ended up being far more successful) would incorporate "of the Dead" and Russo's would adopt "of the Living Dead".

And for the past half-century any filmmaker has been able to make a direct homage to *Night of the Living Dead* without permission and without fear of being sued. Some, such as *Shaun of the Dead* (2004), prove to be very loving tributes.

THE SCENES THAT CHANGED THE LAW

Trading Places *1983*

Movies have a habit of making things up and expecting us to go along with them. That's no earth-shattering revelation, so if you're watching something like *Swordfish* (2001) and expecting it to offer an accurate representation of computer hacking, you're out of luck. Likewise, most of us accept that there's some dramatic licence used when it comes to finance in films. Yet sometimes, an apparently fictional device hits closer to reality than expected.

The scam that underpins *Trading Places* is one of the most potent examples of that. The hit comedy stars Eddie Murphy and Dan Aykroyd, a street hustler and a commodities trader, brought together by antagonists Ralph Bellamy and Don Ameche – the Duke brothers in the movie – as part of a wager to see if the two can swap positions.

The brothers are trying to use insider knowledge to make a lot of quick bucks by betting against the price of frozen concentrated orange juice. To foil the financial crooks, Murphy's and Aykroyd's characters introduce a fake report that suggests the price of the commodity is about to soar. The Duke brothers duly gamble heavily and lose, while Murphy and Aykroyd bet the other way, and make their fortune. The Dukes actually have a cameo appearance in another Murphy film, *Coming to America* (1988), in which we see them begging for money. A neat little crossover, that.

But the ramifications of *Trading Places* go beyond the box office, because the scam perpetrated in the movie could quite easily work in real life. The use of insider trading and information in that sector of the commodities market was not covered by law when *Trading Places* was made, but the Dodd-Frank Wall Street Reform and Consumer Protection Act was signed into US law in 2010 by then-President Barack Obama. In the text of the Act was the "Eddie Murphy Rule", which harks back to the ending of *Trading Places* and specifically outlaws the use of non-public information in order to trade in the futures market. And that's how the ending of a comedy movie alerted authorities to a gap in the law, and ultimately led to its closure.

FROGS AND THE BIBLE

Magnolia *1999*

Paul Thomas Anderson's third film, *Magnolia*, consistently references the numbers 8 and 2. There are around 20 of them in all. Those familiar with the Bible will therefore have got a hint about a major sequence near the end of the film, which we'll come to shortly.

We're told through a still card up front in the movie, for instance, that the weather is "Partly Cloudy, 82% Chance of Rain". In the film's prologue, when the card player needs a 2, they're dealt an 8. The science convention starts at 8.20. The criminal record number for the character of Marcie is 82082082082. The airtanker plane has the number 82 on the side. There are lots more examples, to the point where some fans have worked out that, of the main ten characters in the movie, eight are children and relatives, and two are fathers (and terrible fathers at that).

Furthermore, the word "Exodus" also appears a few times in the background of the movie (on signs by the road), and this points to where the film ultimately goes. Thus, in the Bible book of Exodus, chapter 8 verse 2 reads, "And if thou refuse to let them go, behold. I will smite all thy borders with frogs".

Which, of course, is exactly what happens near the end of *Magnolia*, where frogs are rained down on our characters. Not that raining frogs is an unknown phenomenon. Scientists believe that very strong winds – hurricanes and tornadoes, for instance – can suck small animals up into the sky, and spit them out elsewhere.

An interesting aside: at one stage, a homage to the moment in *Magnolia* where the characters all stop to sing an Aimee Mann song was originally planned for the animated feature *Captain Underpants: The First Epic Movie* (2017). The director, David Soren, was a huge fan of *Magnolia*, so the sequence was storyboarded. However, it didn't, ultimately, fit the film.

I t might seem like a relatively innocuous scene given the film that surrounds it, but there's a moment in Oliver Stone's controversial feature *Natural Born Killers* that had significant ramifications for the product-placement industry.

It's the point where the film shifts tone toward sitcom, in the segment entitled "I Love Mallory". Here, Juliette Lewis's Mallory finds herself in the company of her father, played by Rodney Dangerfield. With the backing of a laughter track, it's a very uneasy piece of cinema which then – in a trick that Stone deploys more than once in the movie – abruptly cuts to a bright and breezy Coca-Cola commercial. If you find it jarring to watch, imagine the reaction of the Coca-Cola Company executives who saw it for the first time without realizing that its use had been officially sanctioned. The company had loosely agreed to allow its advert in the movie, believing that it would feature in a scene where Tommy Lee Jones's prison governor was watching the Superbowl on TV. But it turned out that nobody checked the details properly. Instead, the filmmakers used the commercial to punctuate violent and highly controversial moments in the movie.

The experience triggered an overhaul in product-placement policy from the Coca-Cola Company as well as other big players whose products were sought-after for films. Permissions are more tightly controlled these days but it was too late for *Natural Born Killers*. The permissions were watertight and the scene remains in the movie.

MOMENTS THAT CHANGED MODERN PRODUCT PLACEMENT

Natural Born Killers *1994*

EMPTY ROOMS

The Parallax View *1974*

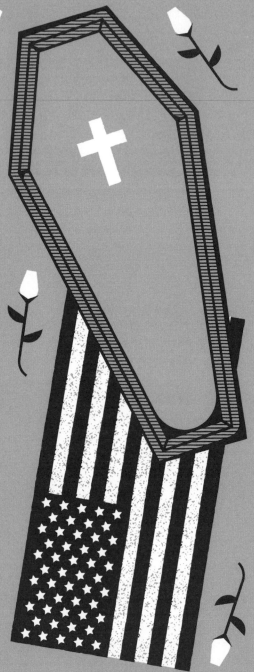

The least-known of Alan J Pakula's loose trilogy of films – *Klute* (1971) and *All the President's Men* (1976) being the other two masterpieces – *The Parallax View* is a humdinger of a political thriller, and one that influenced 1999's underrated *Arlington Road. The Parallax View* itself was informed and influenced by the assassinations of both John F Kennedy and Robert F Kennedy. The opening sequence of the movie – where we witness a presidential candidate being assassinated – is very much a reflection of the latter's murder. From there, the film becomes a taut political thriller, as a reporter digs into the mysterious Parallax Corporation, and discovers that its business is assassination for political gain.

Which all builds to a very haunting ending. A haunting ending that's played out in a big, yet near-empty auditorium. This was at the behest of Pakula, who argued that having few people in the room made the finale all the more effective at getting under your skin as events unravel. The studio, realizing it wouldn't have to fund a room full of extras, quickly agreed to his plan.

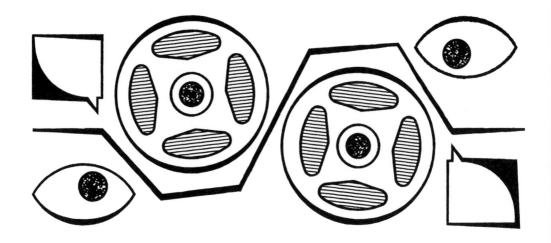

EERILY CLOSE TO THE TRUTH

The Conversation *1974*

Made in the period between the first two *Godfather* movies, Francis Ford Coppola's *The Conversation* is an outstanding thriller, whose reputation continues to bubble up primarily via word of mouth. The film tells the story of a surveillance expert, Harry Caul, played by Gene Hackman, but unbeknownst to Coppola at the time, it had a significant real-life parallel.

On the film's DVD commentary, Coppola revealed that he learned after the fact that the surveillance technology Hackman's character deploys in the film is the same as that used by those in Richard Nixon's administration. It was the tech that, in a way, helped pave the path to the Watergate scandal – and Nixon's resignation from high office. The chronology

is important, though. The script to the film was penned before the Watergate scandal came to light, and principal photography was completed before the bulk of the story broke, so the movie didn't draw on real events.

That aside, *The Conversation* wasn't the easiest shoot. Coppola didn't see eye to eye with his director of photography, Haskell Wexler, and fired him after filming had already begun. He ordered that everything up to that point should be re-shot and brought in Bill Butler to do the job. While his demand was met for most of the material, the surveillance sequence that takes place in Union Square was simply too demanding to be filmed again. It remains the only piece of Wexler's work left in the movie.

HOMAGES, MOTIFS AND CROSS-REFERENCES

Steven Spielberg's 2018 adaptation of Ernest Cline's novel *Ready Player One* was lavish with references to other films. From an extensive recreation of moments from Stanley Kubrick's *The Shining* (1980) – surely one of the most direct homages in blockbuster cinema – through to overt references to a host of other movies from the 1980s and 1990s, it's a film that would hardly exist were it not able to surf on the nostalgia of what's gone before. Sure, the source book has a lot more, but what's interesting about *Ready Player One* is that it's very open about wearing its influences and cultural touch points on its sleeve in plain sight.

But then the blockbuster world around it demands to be fed with some matter. In the internet age, with a growing swarm of websites looking for cross-references in films, movie-makers will play the game to please the fans.

That said, it'd be remiss to call this a new phenomenon. Films have often clambered onto the shoulders – and sometimes the backs – of others to help tell their story. After all, goes the theory, there are only six or seven core stories,

and every tale told since is some variant on one of those. The best storytellers very much bring something of their own to those narratives, of course, often weaving two or three of them together. Guillermo del Toro's sublime *The Shape of Water* (2017) draws heavily, for instance, on *Creature from the Black Lagoon* (1954), and weaves in its references in a way that enhances the story in front of us. (There's a large dose of 1984's *Splash* in there too, many not unreasonably argue.)

Del Toro is also a filmmaker who brings a particular recognisable style to his work (see also page 147), such that if you didn't know who'd made the film you could probably have a solid guess that he was behind it within about 20 minutes of watching. Martin Scorsese and Tim Burton fall into this camp, too.

In this chapter, then, we're going to look at a mix of these things. Those moments in movies that either give broad hints as to who made the film in question, or perhaps offer subtle callbacks to other productions – whether intended overtly or otherwise…

WIRED

BlacKkKlansman *2018*

S pike Lee's richly acclaimed *BlacKkKlansman* features among its cast the American actor Isiah Whitlock Jr., who appears fairly early on in the movie as recruitment agent Mr Turrentine. But the role for which Whitlock Jr. is best known is the corrupt state senator Clay Davis in the sensational TV series *The Wire*. There, his character is notable for uttering the expletive "shit" in a way that stretches the sound out for a good few seconds. Rarely a month goes by when the actor isn't approached by someone in the street asking him to quote this catchphrase.

It turns out that Spike Lee was a fan of Clay Davis, too. So much so that, at the end of his exchange of dialogue in *BlacKkKlansman*, Whitlock Jr. lets out a breath and gives us one last "shiiiiiiiiiiiiiit", for old times' sake…

IT'S MY FILM

Welcome to Marwen *2018*
Back to the Future *1985*

T hroughout *Welcome to Marwen* – a feature film based on the acclaimed 2010 documentary *Marwencol* (*Village of the Dolls* in the UK) – director Robert Zemeckis digs back over three decades of his own career. In a scene in *Welcome to Marwen* that hints at time travel, musical cues from his movie *Back to the Future* are deployed, as well as a familiar pair of blazing trails left behind by the vehicle in the newer film that overtly references the DeLorean from the *Back to the Future* trilogy. Further homages can be found in *Ready Player One* (2018), which includes a Zemeckis Cube (a device that allows time travel) and the *Back to the Future* DeLorean. But then, Zemeckis co-wrote and directed the *Back to the Future* films, and Steven Spielberg was executive producer. If they're not allowed to pay homage to their own productions, then who is?

TELL ME THAT STORY AGAIN

A Bug's Life *1998*
Seven Samurai *1954*
The Magnificent Seven *1960 and 2016*
Battle Beyond the Stars *1980*
Justice League *2017*

Accepting that modern cinema has been infested with remakes, there are films that deliberately go about telling the same story, just in a very different way. Look at the core narrative of Pixar's second feature, *A Bug's Life*. There, the character of Flik goes on a journey to recruit a bunch of warriors to help him defend his home town from a gang of grasshoppers intent on running the place into the ground. While influenced by an Aesop Fable, "The Ant and the Grasshopper", the story is also clearly influenced by Akira Kurosawa's *Seven Samurai*.

Kurosawa's classic film also provided the template for both versions of *The Magnificent Seven*, directed by John Sturges and Antoine Fuqua respectively. Even the low-budget

producer Roger Corman's sci-fi adventure *Battle Beyond the Stars* was effectively a remake of the same story. Ahead of the release of 2017's *Justice League*, meanwhile, its then-director Zack Snyder was open about *Seven Samurai's* direct influence on his tale of a bunch of superheroes being recruited to save the planet.

SYMMETRY

The Grand Budapest Hotel *2014*

Given that the majority of working animators strive for asymmetry when putting their shots together, and that directors consistently look for interesting angles, it's all the more arresting when we find ourselves presented with a symmetrical, widescreen, beautifully composed shot. Whether he's working in live action or animation, Wes Anderson is a master of this approach – to astounding effect.

Look at the establishing shot of the Grand Budapest Hotel in the movie of that name, and how the building itself is absolutely central to the frame. You could put a mirror straight down the middle of the screen and get the same effect. The building you see is itself a physical miniature model, it's one of several shots in the movie – both inside and outside the hotel – where the framing is such that a mirror achieves the same visual.

Examples of this kind of stunning symmetry can be seen throughout Anderson's work but there are particularly fine examples in his 2009 adaptation of Roald Dahl's *Fantastic Mr Fox*. For a beautiful video essay by Kogonada compiling some of these extraordinary shots, visit http://vimeo.com/kogonada/videos.

HAMMER TIME

The Rocky Horror Picture Show *1975*

An affectionate homage to the horror films of British company Hammer Film Productions, *The Rocky Horror Picture Show* pays direct tribute with the sequence where Rocky is brought into the world. One of the most ambitious parts of the film to shoot, this sequence was made difficult by the decision to tip its hat to the style of Hammer films, as well as James Whale's *Frankenstein* (1931). This effect required multiple angles on the same scene – and this was a very low-budget, very stretched production.

But the Hammer love goes deeper than that. *The Rocky Horror Picture Show* uses props from Hammer productions (the tank in the birth scene, for example, was originally used in 1958's *The Revenge of Frankenstein*). The location shooting for Frank-N-Furter's home also took place at Oakley Court, an old house used regularly in Hammer movies including *The Brides of Dracula* (1960) and *The Reptile* (1966).

One more thing you may have noticed. The film's final number, "Super Heroes", mainly bypassed the US release of the film. It was only part of the UK release of the film, although subsequent disc and streaming releases have been complete. It did make it to the official soundtrack album, though.

RELIGIOUS METAPHORS

Superman *1978*
Superman II *1980*
Man of Steel *2013*
RoboCop *1987*
Edward Scissorhands *1990*
Alien 3 *1992*
Cool Hand Luke *1967*
mother! *2017*

The story of Christ has been regularly explored in cinema, with varying degrees of faithfulness to the biblical accounts of his life. But many popular films have also included characters and events that can be seen as metaphors for Christ.

The most obvious is *Superman* and, to a lesser degree, its immediate sequel *Superman II* (both lean on the fact that Superman is the son of a powerful creator – the first film especially). This thread is dispensed with after the first two films, though, only returning in eventual reboot *Man of Steel*, which is much more loaded with religious imagery. That said, the very nature of Superman plays close to the Bible story of Jesus, with a man sending his only son to Earth to live among and bring goodness to humanity.

Perhaps a less obvious metaphor for Jesus is found in the sci-fi classic *RoboCop*. Director Paul Verhoeven admitted that, as far as he's concerned, the film – about a man crucified in the first half and resurrected for the second – is the story of Christ. In fact, there's a moment as the film heads into its final act where a damaged RoboCop appears to be walking on water. That was no accidental shot.

Tim Burton's classic *Edward Scissorhands* can also be seen as a representation of Jesus – a man who tries to bring joy and goodness to the world, only to have the world turn against him. However, this appears to be an argument after the fact rather than Burton's intention (if we're looking for possible inspiration here, *Frankenstein* feels more likely).

It's worth noting David Fincher's much-maligned – perhaps underrated – *Alien 3* as well. Sigourney Weaver's Ellen Ripley lands among a group of religious believers who are fighting an evil force. The religious undertones bubble to the surface in Ripley's moment of ultimate sacrifice at the end of the film: watch how she stretches out her arms in the shape of a cross as she dies, so that those around her can live.

Look, too, to the classic *Cool Hand Luke*. The most famous scene in the film is where prisoner Luke eats 50 eggs (see above). Given that there are 50 prisoners, some have argued that this act represents Luke absorbing their sins. Once he's completed his marathon feast, he lies on the table, arms outstretched in a Christ-like pose.

However, for grand metaphors, take a look at Darren Aronofsky's mightily contentious *mother!*, starring Jennifer Lawrence. While promoting the film, Aronofsky was open about his views that Lawrence was in a way playing "Mother Earth",

representing a planet gradually attacked and stripped back, allowing outsiders into her home. That, or she could be seen as Eve, with her home standing for Eden. Either way, she's powerless as outsiders wreak havoc. Notably, nobody in the film has an explicit name. Javier Bardem's character, for instance, is credited as "Him", which many have speculated suggests a representation of God. This theory is enhanced by the way he's followed by people around the world, and by his overseeing of their home.

Another theory is that Lawrence represents the Virgin Mary, and that her child is therefore Jesus. In addition to that, there's a flood (caused by a broken sink in this case), a book whose message spreads around the world attracting followers, and the wiping of black marks on the foreheads of those who follow the text (which in turn goes back to the idea of Ash Wednesday, and the rubbing of ash on followers' heads). However you read it, there's no doubting the religious subtexts contained within *mother!*.

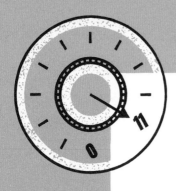

ELEVEN

This Is Spinal Tap *1984*
Deadpool 2 *2018*
Scott Pilgrim vs. the World *2010*

Legendary music mockumentary *This Is Spinal Tap* boasts a famous scene in which the character of Nigel Tufnel explains that his amplifier is special because, unlike all others, his goes up to 11 rather than 10. It's a joke that many films have paid homage to. For instance, in *Deadpool 2*, the gun used by Josh Brolin's Cable also goes to 11. And in Edgar Wright's *Scott Pilgrim vs. the World*, in the crucial amp battle, the Katayanagi twins knock their own amp up to the same level. Even the Internet Movie Database (IMDb) has got in on the fun. The massive online film resource usually invites users to score a film out of 10 stars. In the case of *Spinal Tap*? It's the only film on the service to be allowed an eleventh…

SHARING THE LOOK

The Apartment *1960*
The Crowd *1928*

Billy Wilder's classic *The Apartment* features many brilliant shots, one of which sees Jack Lemmon's Bud Baxter as the only person left working in an office late at night (see above). The office comprises a collection of homogenous-looking desks, in perfectly ordered rows, and with more than $2 million worth of IBM typewriters borrowed to add authenticity to the set.

The origins of this office design lie in a much earlier film. That's because silent movie *The Crowd* (shown above, right) was a touchpoint for art director Alexandre Trauner, whose designs for *The Apartment* were significantly influenced by the look of the 1928 movie.

The Crowd was directed by King Vidor (who reused key characters from it in his 1934 production *Our Daily Bread*). Wilder would pay further homage to the movie in the opening shots of *The Apartment*, including the zoom from the big city into a big office block, and then down to the office floor. It's a stunning shot in both productions.

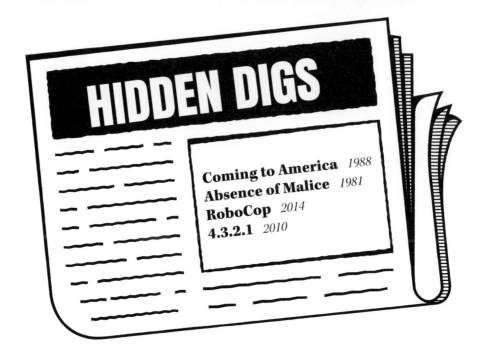

HIDDEN DIGS

Coming to America *1988*
Absence of Malice *1981*
RoboCop *2014*
4.3.2.1 *2010*

While some films take overt pot-shots at big corporations (think of the fast-food outlet McDowell's in *Coming to America* – surprisingly McDonald's didn't take legal action over the similarities), other films are frequently more subtle about the corporate entities that they take issue with.

Sydney Pollack's thriller *Absence of Malice* certainly falls into that category. The film, which earned a trio of Oscar nominations, was penned by Kurt Luedtke alongside an uncredited David Rayfiel, with Paul Newman taking the leading role. Newman was clear that the film was a thinly veiled attack on the *New York Post* newspaper and its page 6 gossip column. *Absence of Malice* tells the story of a naïve young reporter – played by Sally Field – who is manipulated into breaking the news that Newman's character is under investigation for murder, and the court battles that follow.

The 2014 remake of *RoboCop* didn't win an awful lot of friends, but it too wove in some sly digs through the scrolling news stories at the bottom of the live TV reports. Look out for lines such as "Green Peace attacked by WikiLeaks hackers", "Mexican President opposes illegal Americans" and "President gives okay for astronauts to take hookers to space".

British director – and Liverpool Football Club fan – Noel Clarke also made use of scrolling news reports in *4.3.2.1.* to make clear his sporting preferences, declaring "Chelsea Football Club declared bankrupt", among other stories.

THE FILM THAT HELPED SHAPE STAR WARS

The Hidden Fortress *1958*
Star Wars: A New Hope *1977*

George Lucas has cited several influences that inspired him to put together the first *Star Wars* film. He's openly acknowledged that a key one was Akira Kurosawa's 1958 classic, *The Hidden Fortress*. What particularly interested Lucas about the film, and something he ultimately paid homage to in the first of his franchise, was the idea of telling the story from the perspective of two small, apparently unimportant characters in the film's world. In the case of *Star Wars: A New Hope*, those characters are, of course, the droids R2-D2 and C-3PO. The characters of Princess Leia and Han Solo were also partly inspired by Kurosawa's movie, based on Princess Yuki and – very, very loosely – Hyoe Tadokoro respectively.

Even the legendary Death Star trench run at the end of *Star Wars: A New Hope* is an homage to a scene in *The Hidden Fortress* in which a general charges on horseback amid scenes of chaos and destruction all around him. YouTubers have pieced together side-by-side comparisons of key scenes from both films, and there are sizeable crossovers throughout Lucas's original trilogy.

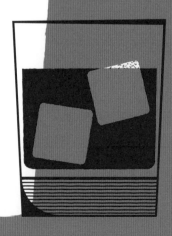

OLD FRIENDS

Arthur *1981*

Dudley Moore's long-time comedy partner Peter Cook was said to have been the part-inspiration for one of his most famous and successful movie roles, playing Arthur Bach in the double-Oscar-winning comedy *Arthur*. Cook's drinking had got in the way of their partnership toward the end of their time working together, and led to the duo falling out. Moore carried that into the role of Arthur, basing the character's behaviour in part on how he'd seen Cook act once the drink had taken hold.

THE CLASSIC THAT INSPIRED A BLOCKBUSTER

The Wizard of Oz *1939*
Twister *1996*

The influences of *The Wizard of Oz* (shown above) are worn proudly on the sleeves of weather/flying-cow blockbuster *Twister*, and director Jan de Bont openly stated that he drew on the tornado sequence in the 1939 classic for his own movie. That's why in *Twister* you'll find the scientific device that the characters use named after Dorothy – there's even a painting of her on the side of it.

The computer-generated weather effects in *Twister* also pay homage to *The Wizard of Oz*. De Bont was amazed by how convincing the scene looked back in 1939, and pushed his effects team to hit that standard. All of this was with good reason, too, as the tornado sequence in *The Wizard of Oz* is a marvel of early special-effects ingenuity.

To create the on-screen illusion, the crew – inspired by the wind socks used at airports – crafted a muslin stocking more than 10 metres (33 feet) long, which they wrapped around chicken wire to give it the shape of a tornado. This was attached to a car that travelled along a track off-screen to move the "twister" around. The rest of the stormy scene was filled in using a wind machine, miniature work and paintings.

FRAMES PER SECOND

Mission: Impossible II *2000*
Hard Boiled *1992*
The Killer *1989*
Face/Off *1997*
Windtalkers *2002*
Broken Arrow *1996*

John Woo's slow-motion sequences have become a stunning trademark of one of the world's most accomplished action directors – an effect he uses to heighten what he considers important dramatic moments in his films. To achieve that effect, Woo ups the frames-per-second rate, and thus slows the footage down on screen.

Woo says that he adapts the frame rate depending on the performer, too. For instance, on *Mission: Impossible II*, Tom Cruise allowed Woo to crank up the frame rate as high as he could: 120 frames per second. Regular Woo collaborator Yun-fat Chow, star of stunning action movies *Hard Boiled* (shown left) and *The Killer*, was also shot at 120 frames per second.

To get such a high frame rate requires the actors' movements to be fluid – almost balletic. The slightest imperfection would show up clearly at such a rate. In fact, any increase in frame rate is some achievement for a performer. Woo has revealed that on *Face/Off*, he filmed Nicolas Cage sometimes at 60 frames per second, sometimes 96 (and the same again with *Windtalkers*). John Travolta, was also shot at 96 for both *Face/Off* and his previous Woo collaboration, *Broken Arrow* (Travolta's rhythmic dancing background standing him in very good stead). Across both his Hong Kong and Hollywood films, this has become Woo's signature style.

SCREEN-SPLITTING AND LONG SHOTS

Sisters *1973*
Carrie *1976*
Blow Out *1981*
Snake Eyes *1998*

Director Brian De Palma frequently pays homage to director Alfred Hitchcock in his work. But he also has a signature style of his own, most notably involving a split-screen effect. In *Sisters*, for instance, this effect allows him to contrast the actions of one character with another by slicing up his screen (as shown above). He equally adeptly uses the technique in his adaptation of Stephen King's horror classic *Carrie*. For the climactic sequence of the title character at the prom, he builds and builds and builds the split screen, mixing it in with a variety of effects, including close-ups, quick edits, slow motion and changes of perspective, before the tension is allowed to pop – to devastating effect.

Split screen isn't a feature of every De Palma movie, but it is put to effect in *Blow Out* and *Snake Eyes*. As an added bonus in *Snake Eyes*, take a look at the extended opening tracking shot. It looks like a continuous 13-minute take, but De Palma hides a couple of cuts in there that are devilishly hard to spot. For example, watch as De Palma's writing credit appears on screen. You might spot a character walk across the frame in the foreground. It's a "blink and you miss it" cut, but it's definitely there.

EMULATING HITCHCOCK

Vertigo *1958*
Jaws *1975*
Goodfellas *1990*

For *Vertigo*, director Alfred Hitchcock and second unit director of photography Irmin Roberts deployed a type of ground-breaking shot that has been heavily mimicked ever since. It's known as the dolly zoom, and in *Vertigo* (shown above), we see it used to amplify the terror on the face of John "Scottie" Ferguson (played by James Stewart) as he ascends stairs, then looks down. The foreground of the shot remains the same, but the background stretches backward. It's a shot achieved by the camera pulling away but the lens of its gaze zooming in.

Several directors have paid homage to this. In *Jaws*, Chief Brody (Roy Scheider) is sitting down on a deckchair overseeing the beach when he realizes there's a shark in the water, and the terror quickly engulfs him. Director Steven Spielberg uses one of cinema's most famous dolly zoom shots to hammer home just when the realization of what's happening hits Brody.

Martin Scorsese uses it more subtly toward the end of *Goodfellas*, as Robert De Niro's Jimmy and Ray Liotta's Henry Hill meet at an everyday diner in one of the film's climactic scenes. Scorsese never lets the viewer settle on them, and uses dolly zooms to move us in and out as the scene progresses – a small tribute to *Vertigo*, where the effect was first used.

LONG TAKES

The Shape of Water *2017*
Mimic *1997*

The Best Picture Oscar-winning fantasy *The Shape of Water* is a masterclass in the long takes that its director and co-writer, Guillermo del Toro, had been evolving for the two decades before the film's release.

Del Toro has freely admitted that the turning point in his career was the production, 20 years before, of the movie *Mimic*, made for the Weinstein siblings – the now-disgraced Harvey and his brother Bob. Bob in particular heavily interfered with the movie, and one consequence of this was that del Toro adapted his style and process for his subsequent films to ensure that no one could ever take the guts of his stories away from him again. It's why you see so many long shots in del Toro movies. They're both beautiful and so long that an interfering studio executive wouldn't be able to cut them.

He achieved this by starting to edit his movies as he went along (one of the first of a now-growing number of directors to adopt this practice), generally having a first cut ready a week after production had wrapped. But also, as he told the *Independent* newspaper: "I learned to make my camera more fluid, more a storytelling character; it really helped me develop the language that now I practice on *The Shape of Water*. It taught me to edit every day because I was always expecting to be fired."

The long takes that del Toro employs, therefore, not only weave the camera into the story a lot more, but also make it virtually impossible for someone to hack around later on. If he'd continued with the shorter takes that are more evident in *Mimic*, it'd be far easier for an executive to ask for things to be removed.

PAYING TRIBUTE TO SILENT CINEMA

Mad Max *1979*
Despicable Me *2010–17*
Jackass Number Two *2006*
Steamboat Bill, Jr. *1928*
Project A Part II *1987*

It may not be the most obvious link, but among the key influences on the ultra-violent action film *Mad Max* were the silent movies of stars such as Buster Keaton and Harold Lloyd. Not specific scenes, but the universality of their language – the fact that they relied heavily on what you could see, rather than what you could hear. In fact, director and co-writer George Miller would describe the first *Mad Max* film – one he didn't particularly enjoy making – as "a silent movie with sound".

The work of Buster Keaton, regarded by many as the finest comedy performer of the silent era, continues to ripple through cinema. The creators of the Minions from the *Despicable Me* series have been open about the fact that their hugely popular critters pay deliberate homage to the likes of Keaton and Charlie Chaplin through the physicality of their comedy.

Even more directly, Johnny Knoxville has attributed the moment in *Jackass Number Two*

where the façade of a saloon falls over him as a direct homage to the 1928 film *Steamboat Bill, Jr.* (shown above). For Knoxville, though, the stunt that occurs in *Jackass Number Two* nearly went badly wrong. The idea was that the window would pass over his head as the house front collapsed on him. His head did make it through, but on one take his body took a sizeable hit. A few inches either side, it would have hit Knoxville's head and killed him. At least the house that fell on Knoxville was made of relatively light materials. In Keaton's original, the building was bricks and mortar. If any of it had hit the actor he probably wouldn't have survived to tell the tale.

Jackie Chan is also a huge fan of *Steamboat Bill, Jr.*, and he paid homage to that final house scene by recreating it in his film *Project A Part II*. Unusually for Chan, a stuntman and martial artist as well as an actor and director, he made it through the stunt pretty much unscathed.

MISSION: IMPOSSIBLE

The vault heist scene in *Mission: Impossible* (1996; shown opposite) is, like much of Brian De Palma's work, a tip of the hat to classic movies of times past. It includes some taxing moments for Tom Cruise. Let's take a look…

1 The scene pays deliberate homage to the little-heard-of 1964 heist movie *Topkapi* (1964), directed by Jules Dassin. *Topkapi* includes Gilles Segal among its ensemble cast, and he undertakes wire stunts that are clear inspirations for Tom Cruise's descent into the Langley vault here. In addition, the sequence has parallels with the classic heist movie *Rififi* (1955), also directed by Dassin, but it's *Topkapi* that's the real influence.

2 What you don't see in this scene is that in order to maintain body balance, Cruise had to come up with something to counteract the fact that heads are heavier than feet. The solution was a simple one: he apparently put coins in his shoes.

3 As usual, it is Cruise himself who undertakes the stunt (see also More Pain on page 52). In subsequent *Mission: Impossible* films he also performs the centrepiece action, rather than relying on stunt performers and doubles. Most notably, these have seen him hanging off the side of Dead Horse Point (*Mission: Impossible II,* 2000), climbing the world's tallest building, the Burj Khalifa (*Mission: Impossible – Ghost Protocol,* 2011), and clinging to a plane as it takes off (*Mission: Impossible – Rogue Nation,* 2015).

4 The overhead shot of Cruise being lowered into the vault, which precedes the scene shown opposite, can be seen as a direct homage to a similar shot in Stanley Kubrick's *2001: A Space Odyssey* (1968).

5 What you can't tell from this picture is that this is the only major set-piece in the *Mission: Impossible* franchise with no music. Instead, director De Palma opts

for pretty much silence, cutting out Danny Elfman's backing score in the highest-tension scene of the film.

6 Unusually for a key moment of high drama in a blockbuster movie, the scene uses many long takes. This is a style De Palma employs regularly (as we have already seen on page 145), for which he was heavily influenced by the directorial style of Alfred Hitchcock (Hitchcock, in fact, composed an entire film – *Rope*, 1948 – out of long takes, only zooming in on something to obviously cut when his camera ran out of film). The longer takes, against steady silence, contribute to making the Langley vault heist one of the most-mimicked blockbuster scenes of the 1990s.

One more aside. Next time you watch *Mission: Impossible*, go through the opening credits again. Few big Hollywood movies have given away, in plain sight, so many plot moments from the film you're about to watch...

MELINA MERCOURI   PETER USTINOV   MAXIMILIAN SCHELL

"We're crooks (honest)! We resolve to make the world a better place to steal in!"

THE MAN-LOVER   THE ELECTRONICS GENIUS   THE MASTERMIND   THE SCHMO

Topkapi
(where the jewels *were* are!)

Join us in Istanbul— we'll cut you in on the theft of the century!

ROBERT MORLEY
AKIM TAMIROFF
Screenplay by MONJA DANISCHEWSKY, ERIC AMBLER
Music by MANOS HADJIDAKIS
Directed by JULES DASSIN   COLOR
UNITED ARTISTS

BE THERE ON TIME— WE'D HATE TO START WITHOUT YOU!

SETS AND LOCATIONS

While the headlines surrounding Hollywood movies in particular tend to talk about the tens of millions of dollars – plus change – being lavished on productions, when it gets down to the nitty-gritty of physical filming, ingenuity and cost management still have an integral part to play. After all, a movie star may take home a pretty penny for their work, but the props department still often has to function on a fairly frugal allocation.

Sometimes, too, it simply makes sense to share resources. Studios such as Paramount and Warner Bros., for instance, have massive backlots in Los Angeles, full of sets that they only need to build once. Sure, they can be dressed differently to tell different stories, but they're still ostensibly the same construction. Thus, on the Warner Bros. backlot is a set called New York Street. The hotel on that street was used in *Blade Runner* (1982), but it's also the same building outside which Jim Carrey sang "Cuban Pete" in 1994's *The Mask*.

Also on the New York-themed area of the Warner backlot is a fire escape that was host to the infamous kiss in 2002's *Spider-Man* movie. That same set was used in the hugely expensive staging of the musical *Annie*, back in 1982.

Paramount Pictures, a short way across town from Warner Bros., also has a New York set. To give you a flavour of the different films that make use of the exact same location, *Cloverfield* (2008) shot extensively on it, as did Best Picture Oscar winner *The Artist* (2011). Going right back, 1961's classic *Breakfast at Tiffany's* filmed in the same physical outside set (although it's been overhauled several times since). Even if you watch all these films closely, you still might not be able to tell that you're looking at pretty much the same thing. Yet you are.

Not all of these sets have been used with permission, either. When the budget ran out on the 1967 Sonny and Cher musical comedy *Good Times*, its director – William Friedkin – had an idea. He took his cameraman onto the Paramount lot, where the security guard let them in, unaware that Friedkin's production office there had shut down the week before, and captured footage in plain sight – including using the set where TV show *Bonanza* had been filming. Friedkin thus managed to complete his film without completely blowing the budget.

Movie sets and locations, then, hold no shortage of stories in and of themselves, which is what we're going to look at in this very chapter...

IT'S HOT OUT HERE...

Do the Right Thing *1989*

Spike Lee's superb debut comedy-drama feature *Do the Right Thing* (shown above) is set over the course of one very hot summer day in a Brooklyn neighbourhood, in New York City. Lee shot the film on location in Brooklyn, building sets for the pizza place and Korean grocery store in empty lots on the street. Unfortunately, the temperature wasn't quite as high as the film required for authenticity. Production designer Wynn Thomas had a brainwave, making the walls of the buildings look "warmer" by deploying large quantities of red and orange paint to fool viewers into thinking that it was hotter than it actually was. The ploy worked a treat.

A DIFFERENT GAME

Ralph Breaks the Internet *2018*

The moment in this Disney sequel where Ralph and Vanellope visit the Oh My Disney website was in fact a substitute for the original plan. In a moment of what posh marketing people call "synergy", filmmakers had originally decided that the pair would visit the Disney Infinity videogame, for which the Disney Princesses sequence was originally designed. However, during production, Disney cancelled the videogame after three versions (and the release of umpteen collectable figures to work with it), and as such, a rework was required. Hence the appearance of the Oh My Disney location in the film, awash with Disney-owned characters and brands. The Princesses were carried over.

TIME AND DATE

1984 *1984*

George Orwell wrote his future dystopia *Nineteen Eighty-Four* back in the year 1948, coming up with the title and era by reversing the two numbers at the end of the date. Writer/director Michael Radford brought to the screen arguably the most acclaimed version of the story, with John Hurt in the lead role of Winston Smith. As future-driven as the setting may sometimes look, though, the film came together in quite a rush in the end, as the plan was to shoot it in the same year and the same geographical area where Orwell had set his tale. But that's not fully what you see. As it turned out, most of the movie was shot on studio sets, with exterior photography at Beckton Gasworks in London. In fact, the film crossed over a few locations with Terry Gilliam's *Brazil* (1985), which was filming at the same time.

Another notable feature of this film is that the anthems you hear throughout are deliberately all in a major key. That's because Radford felt that left-wing tyrannies all have their anthems in a minor key, whereas right-wing tyrannies opt for a major key. The Big Brother regime falls very much into the latter camp, so a major key was selected for the film.

DESTROYED AFTER USE

West Side Story *1961*
Lethal Weapon 3 *1992*
Brazil *1985*

In his memoir, actor Danny Aiello revealed his particular affection for the brilliant *West Side Story*, and the area of New York in which it's shot. The film's location had a particular poignancy for Aiello. For authenticity, much of the movie was shot in run-down, abandoned Manhattan apartments in the area that Aiello grew up in. The production was the last to make use of them – shortly after filming wrapped, these buildings were pulled down, with the classic film a lasting monument to them.

Film producers often seize the opportunities offered by structures that are up for demolition. For example, the opening sequence of *Lethal Weapon 3* is centred on the destruction of a building. The producers were tipped off that it was set to be pulled down, and the opening of the movie was duly written around its demise (note that it's worth sitting through the end credits for a final hidden gag that very neatly bookends the film).

Terry Gilliam's classic sci-fi film *Brazil*, meanwhile, was seeking a look whereby – to paraphrase Gilliam's own words – the century was compacted into a single moment. That meant filming across Europe, and the location for protagonist Sam Lowry's apartment was actually Marne-la-Vallée in France. Not long after filming had wrapped, that very same site became the home of Disneyland Paris. There's no parallel at all to be drawn between a film concerning itself with technology problems and consumerism, and one of Europe's biggest heavily branded theme parks...

EATEN BY THE DESERT

Star Wars prequel trilogy *1999–2005*

When George Lucas was looking to film his trilogy of *Star Wars* prequel movies, starting with *The Phantom Menace* (1999), he was keen to find a desert location to create the small town of Mos Espa on the planet Tatooine, where we first meet a young Anakin Skywalker. Lucas settled on Tunisia, and around 20 buildings were put up in an area on the cusp of the Sahara Desert for the movie. Those locations were also used in *Attack of the Clones* (2002). Unusually, after filming ended, the sets were left standing.

As such, the world of Mos Espa that you see on screen became something of a tourist attraction, bringing a boost to the local economy.

After more than 15 years, though, most of the set – located just north-west of the city of Tozeur – has fallen prey to the elements, abandoned to the hostility of the Sahara Desert. The shifting sands of the area are gradually engulfing the construction, leading to the disappearance of the sets and the steady stream of tourists.

WE'LL REUSE THAT, THANK YOU

Aliens *1986*
Batman *1989*
Dark City *1998*
The Matrix *1999*
Carry On Cleo *1964*
Cleopatra *1963*

There are many notable examples of big-budget productions reusing sets from earlier films, as Hollywood studios look to make the most of their previous investments.

Take the link between *Aliens* (shown opposite, top) and *Batman* (inset opposite), both of which were shot at Pinewood Studios in London. For *Aliens*, a set was constructed for the "Atmosphere Processor". It wasn't taken apart after filming and was happened upon by Tim Burton during pre-production on *Batman*. It thus found a second use as a key part of the Axis Chemicals plant in his movie, where Jack Nicholson's Jack Napier is transformed into the Joker.

Two key science-fiction films of the 1990s also used the same set as one another. *Dark City* and *The Matrix* were using Fox Studios in Australia just a year apart, and the latter made good use of structures built for the former. The rooftop sequences in *The Matrix*, in particular, will look familiar to those who've seen *Dark City*.

But the prize for the most deliberately brazen reuse of sets has to go to 1964's *Carry On Cleo*.

The comedy spoof on the story of Antony and Cleopatra was timed pretty much to perfection. The year before its release, Fox's hugely expensive production *Cleopatra*, starring Elizabeth Taylor and Richard Burton, had arrived in cinemas and the *Carry On Cleo* movie reused many of the sets from the earlier film. But that wasn't all. *Carry On Cleo* stars Sid James and Amanda Barrie even wore the costumes that had been made for Burton and Taylor in *Cleopatra*.

However, the set for *Carry On Cleo* still led to a surprising legal problem. British high street store

Marks & Spencer wasn't impressed with a sign for slave traders called Marcus et Spencius which also used the store's colour scheme. A legal threat ensued, which was ultimately settled by *Carry On Cleo* producer Peter Rogers penning a letter of apology. The sign remains in the film.

THE REUSED COCKPIT

Executive Decision *1996*
Air Force One *1997*

Take two 1990s action films that both enjoyed success at the box office. *Executive Decision*, headlined by Kurt Russell and (temporarily) Steven Seagal, came first, and then Harrison Ford scored one of the biggest non-*Star Wars/Indiana Jones* hits of his career with president-on-a-plane flick *Air Force One*. What's the connection, you wonder? Despite being made by completely different companies and filmmakers, they shared a central resource: the cockpit of the plane in both films is one and the same.

The set used for *Executive Decision* was re-dressed and appears a bit different in *Air Force One*, but if you're looking for a telltale sign, consider this: both sets were based on a Boeing 747-200 aircraft, which by design did not have an all-glass cockpit. And yet the planes in both *Executive Decision* and *Air Force One* both have one – a concession to the needs of filming and added drama, no doubt, but also evidence that you're looking at the very same airplane innards.

THE MYSTERY OF THE LOST PAINTING

Stuart Little *1999*

As well as being co-written by *The Sixth Sense*'s M Night Shyamalan, the screen adaptation of *Stuart Little* also managed to resolve a missing-picture mystery.

The production team were on the hunt for details to dress the background set of the Littles' home. They found a painting they liked in an antique store, bought it for a reported $500, and hung it on their set (it can be seen behind the Littles, above). What the team didn't know was that they'd actually rediscovered a long-lost 1920s painting by Hungarian artist Róbert Berény. It was only when art historian Gergely Barki happened to be watching the movie on TV with his young daughter – a decade after its release – and caught sight of the picture that this came to light. Barki was surprised and excited to see the painting hanging prominently on the wall in the movie, and quickly contacted the production company to track the painting down.

It turned out that it had been sold to a private collector after the film had wrapped. A very lucky private collector. Barki's enthusiasm led to the rediscovery of what was considered a lost masterpiece, which sold for the best part of £200,000 at auction in 2014. It goes by the self-explanatory title of "Sleeping Lady With Black Vase" if you want to keep a look-out for it.

BURNING DOWN OTHER SETS

Gone With the Wind *1939*

One of the most famous scenes in the classic *Gone With the Wind* – the burning of Atlanta – was an ambitious sequence that required resources from other productions to fully realize. It was shot on the Selznick International backlot, leased from RKO Pictures and known at the time as "The Back Forty". Located in Culver City, California, the lot played host to many famous outdoor sets before it was ultimately demolished in 1976.

That said, the production of *Gone With the Wind* had demolished many of those sets long before the gates were closed for the last time. The burning of Atlanta sequence was bulked up by the torching of several old sets on the backlot that were no longer required. Most famously,

the set for the 1933 classic version of *King Kong* is there, burning to ash before your very eyes as Scarlett and Rhett make their way through the chaos.

The burning of Atlanta was the first big set sequence filmed for the movie. Only once the ashes had cooled down and had been cleaned up could further sets for the production be built on the same ground.

Furthermore, at the time it was filmed the movie's co-star, Vivien Leigh, hadn't even been cast as Scarlett. Filmmakers used a stunt double for her character – a double who was chosen despite not knowing the actress she would be doubling for.

HOLY GROUND

Monty Python's Life of Brian *1979*
Jesus of Nazareth *1977*

T here wasn't a huge amount of money in the pot to make the classic *Monty Python's Life of Brian* (shown top right) and they managed to stretch that budget by shifting filming to Tunisia (not long after the first *Star Wars* film had shot in the area – see page 157). But look closely at the *Life of Brian* sets, and you might recognize them from the television mini-series *Jesus of Nazareth* (shown below right), which was overseen by director Franco Zeffirelli. Two years later, the Python team opted to use many of the sets and costumes from the previous production in their film (although some sets were still built specially for *Life of Brian*).

A problem did present itself, at the point in the movie when the character of Brian goes to the window and accidentally shows off his nether regions to the crowd outside. Graham Chapman, who played Brian, wasn't circumcised and, in the words of director Terry Jones: "We can see you're not Jewish!" What you actually see in the film, then, is Chapman wearing a rubber band to achieve the required effect!

SPIELBERG'S TAKE ON THE FUTURE

Minority Report *2002*
Ready Player One *2018*

Considering the film was set in the future at the time it was made, what's interesting about the look of Steven Spielberg's *Minority Report* (shown above) is how old the architecture on display is. Sure, it's overlaid with graphics and computer-generated visuals, but the physical buildings themselves bear little sign of modernity. The same applies to sequences in his 2018 adaptation of Ernest Cline's *Ready Player One*. There, Spielberg was looking for a location that painted a picture of a miserable, run-down future, just a few decades in the future. He settled on Birmingham, in the West Midlands.

These decisions were, as you might suspect, a deliberate choice. The thinking on *Minority Report* came from Spielberg himself. He argued – along with production designer Alex McDowell – that the buildings we live in today are sometimes 100 years old; that the modern world isn't full of bizarre sci-fi buildings, it's just bricks and mortar that have stood the test of time. *Minority Report*'s one concession was to make those existing buildings appear a bit grubbier. But under the gloss of the film, they're contemporary structures.

While we're here, *Minority Report* wasn't a film to shy away from product placement – in fact, it actually funded a large part of the movie. Toyota was keen to showcase its brand of luxury car, the Lexus, and stumped up a cool $5 million to see it featured in Spielberg's futuristic world. Nokia chipped in another $2 million. In all, around a quarter of the film's physical production budget was funded by such deals.

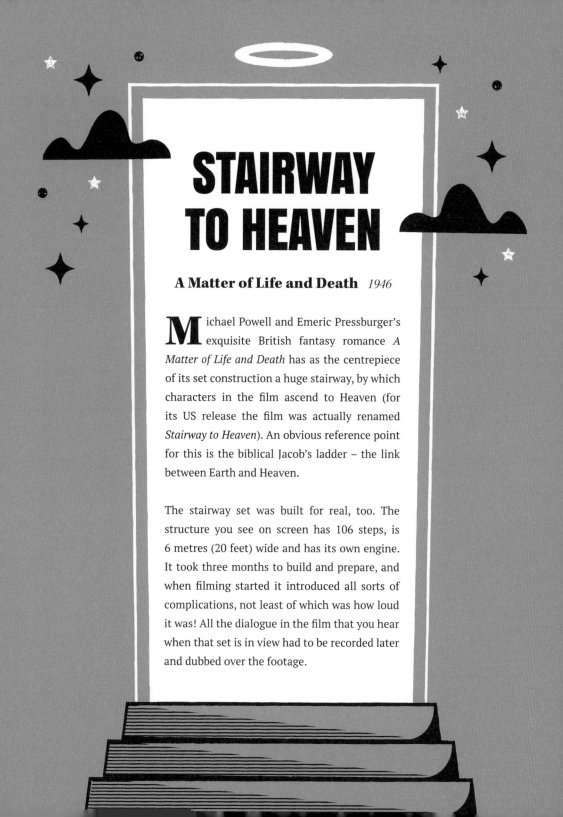

STAIRWAY TO HEAVEN

A Matter of Life and Death *1946*

Michael Powell and Emeric Pressburger's exquisite British fantasy romance *A Matter of Life and Death* has as the centrepiece of its set construction a huge stairway, by which characters in the film ascend to Heaven (for its US release the film was actually renamed *Stairway to Heaven*). An obvious reference point for this is the biblical Jacob's ladder – the link between Earth and Heaven.

The stairway set was built for real, too. The structure you see on screen has 106 steps, is 6 metres (20 feet) wide and has its own engine. It took three months to build and prepare, and when filming started it introduced all sorts of complications, not least of which was how loud it was! All the dialogue in the film that you hear when that set is in view had to be recorded later and dubbed over the footage.

THE LOCATION THAT HELPED MAKE THE FILM

The Truman Show *1998*

Providing a breakthrough role for Jim Carrey, who proved he could headline far more than comedies, *The Truman Show* can also lay claim to being one of the most prescient Hollywood movies of the 1990s. The reality television explosion would begin within 12 months of the film's release.

The filmmakers knew the importance of careful planning when it came to Seahaven – the town where the character of Truman lives under the constant gaze of hidden cameras. They looked at creating the town on a studio backlot, but in the end filming took place in a real town. Seaside, in Florida, was planned, designed and built in the 1940s to have the look of an old-fashioned town. It's a rather curious place; if you look closely, you'll see that all the houses are built to three-quarters scale, and you'll never see the same fence twice on a street. Every single house has a porch. In fact, the only set-building work required was for Truman's office, which itself was annexed to an existing building. Everything else? Real. Director Peter Weir has always maintained that the discovery of the town of Seaside was pivotal to the success of *The Truman Show.*

One other key ingredient in the film is Ed Harris, in the role of overseer Christof. In fact, Dennis Hopper was originally cast for this part, but a day into his work, he and director Peter Weir agreed to part ways, which meant the film had a casting hole in it with production already underway. Ed Harris was duly drafted in with only a few days to prepare for the role. This change was only possible because all the material involving Christof was to be shot at the end of production. Again, look closely – none of the Christof material is set in Seahaven; it's all studio-set.

IS THAT METROPOLIS?

Top Secret! *1984*

The superb spoof movie *Top Secret!* was made by the team of Zucker-Abrahams-Zucker (ZAZ) in between their far higher profile projects *Airplane!* (1980) and *The Naked Gun* (1988). But *Top Secret!* is the equal of both.

There's a moment in this film of particular geeky appeal. It's the scene where Lucy Gutteridge's Hillary Flammond looks down from her balcony at the street below, on which we suddenly see mice and hamsters walking along – the joke being that it's a miniature set. But what's of note here is that it's actually a recycled set. It was originally used in 1978's *Superman*, and the filmmakers discovered it while working at Shepperton Studios in England. They vowed to squeeze the set into their new film, and duly did.

There are often hidden jokes in the film too, even extending to the German phrases littered throughout. For instance, when the train is pulling out of the checkpoint near the start of the film, the situation announcer says, "Der Zug der jetzt auf Gleis drei steht... hat uns alle überrascht". The translation for this? "The train now on platform three... surprised us all."

I KNOW THAT ALLEY

Harry Potter *2001–2011*
Les Misérables *2012*

Considering it's one of the most-watched collections in contemporary movie history, it's surprising when work that appears in the *Harry Potter* series of films crops up in a completely different production without too many people noticing. However, that was the case with the Diagon Alley set (shown below), which was reused in the Oscar-winning film adaptation of the musical *Les Misérables* (below right). It may have been re-dressed, but look closely at the ABC Café and barricade set in *Les Mis* and it's just about recognizable.

Another thing to look out for in *Les Misérables*. There's a scene in a factory where Anne Hathaway's Fantine is making rosary beads. These beads are quite noisy when knocked together in real life – and certainly in the context of a film set, where silence is often crucial at key moments. Production designer Eve Stewart came up with a clever solution: she coated the beads in rubber. In fact, rubber was used quite a lot on the set of *Les Misérables*, including to coat the shoes of the horses to minimize the noise of their footsteps.

THE FRANKENSTEIN SET

Independence Day *1996*

Much of the budget for the gigantic blockbuster *Independence Day* had been allocated to the special effects and incredible model work. When it came to building the sets, therefore, dollars needed to be stretched, so filmmakers pulled in assets from a mix of differing productions.

The White House set that you see in the film had already appeared in two 1995 movies: the romantic comedy *The American President* – the film that was the catalyst for the hugely successful TV show *The West Wing* – and Oliver Stone's *Nixon* biopic. And the same set went on to appear in *Mars Attacks!* (1996), whose release was delayed partly in response to the success of

Independence Day. On the DVD commentary for the film, it's revealed that some interiors of the stealth bombers and submarines were reused from *Broken Arrow* (1996) and *Crimson Tide* (1995) respectively. Even the dog in the film had popped up before, in *Far From Home: The Adventures of Yellow Dog* (1995).

A further fact about the vehicles. Filmmakers had to draft in external experts to help them accurately portray the military vehicles in the movie, after the US military withdrew support for the film. It had originally agreed to provide assistance, but only on condition that any references to Area 51 were removed from the film. The filmmakers declined this condition.

LOTS AND LOTS OF SETS

The Shining *1980*
Oliver! *1968*
Scrooge *1970*

When Stanley Kubrick was filming *The Shining*, he was characteristically precise about how things should be done. He wanted the flexibility to film on any set at any time. As such, all the extensive interior sets for the movie were constantly standing, preventing any other production from filming at Elstree Studios in London. This, together with Kubrick's exhaustive filming process, had a knock-on effect on other productions that were waiting to use the space – *Raiders of the Lost Ark* (1981) among them.

For the filming of the musical *Oliver!*, pretty much the entirety of Shepperton Studios in Surrey, England, was taken up. Furthermore, even though it may not appear so on film, much of the movie was shot on the backlot in the open air. The song and dance routine to "Consider Yourself" took three weeks to film and was one of many that make use of several different sets if you watch closely.

In fact, you might recognize those sets if you happen to switch on *Scrooge*, starring Albert Finney. That too was shot at Shepperton, and the *Oliver!* sets were extensively redeployed as part of that production. Charles Dickens would have approved...

THE ORIGINS OF A GIANT SHIP

The Goonies *1985*

I t's a fairly well-known story that director Richard Donner held back the reveal of the pirate ship (shown above) from his young cast when filming *The Goonies*, wanting to capture their genuine reactions when they saw something this incredible for the first time. It's safe to say he got his wish: the look on their faces when they do see it is the real deal.

The ship itself, the *Inferno*, was directly influenced by the vessel seen on screen in the Errol Flynn-headlined picture *The Sea Hawk* (1940). An early hint at that connection is a scene in *The Goonies*

where the character of Sloth is watching a pirate film on television. That film is indeed *The Sea Hawk*, and the ships in both pictures are really quite similar – deliberately so.

The Goonies's boat also owed something to Pirates of the Caribbean – not the films, but the theme park ride at Disneyland. The ride was going through renovations when *The Goonies* was being shot, so the filmmakers were able to use some of its rigging on their set. The Disneyland ride went on to inspire a successful film franchise some 15 years later, of course.

SKYFALL

The first James Bond film to cross $1 billion at the global box office, *Skyfall* (2012) was actually downscaled geographically after facing delays and financial difficulties from one of the studios involved. That's why it's got a very British feel to it, beyond the usual UK trappings of a 007 movie.

1 *Skyfall* director Sam Mendes cited Christopher Nolan's *The Dark Knight* trilogy, and in particular 2008's *The Dark Knight*, as a big influence on his first 007 movie. Mendes was impressed that Nolan was able to make a "huge movie that is thrilling and entertaining, and has a lot to say about the world we live in", all in the midst of a Batman story. The *Skyfall* shot pictured opposite directly reflects the one in *The Dark Knight* in which Christian Bale's Batman is surveying the Gotham cityscape.

2 The building that 007 is seen standing on opposite is that of the UK's one-time Department for Energy and Climate Change (a now-defunct government department). In order to get the necessary elevation to capture the shot Mendes was after, scaffolding was used to add 1 metre (3 feet) to the height of the roof.

3 The building in the foreground of the picture shown opposite – and it's hard to think this is a coincidence – is the old War Office. This structure had served as the MI6 HQ in three previous 007 adventures from the 1980s: *Licence to Kill*, *A View to a Kill* and *Octopussy*.

4 The bulk of *Skyfall* is set, unusually for a James Bond saga, in the UK. In particular, London and Glencoe, in Scotland. The reason for this is that the film was hit by parent studio MGM's financial instability – and was even put on hold for around eight months while financing was sorted. As a result, it was decided to zero in on Britain more as a location, as it would be more economic to do so (the only other countries visited for the shoot were China, Turkey and Japan). The next Bond film, *Spectre* (2015), was gifted with a far more substantive budget, which allowed it to travel the world.

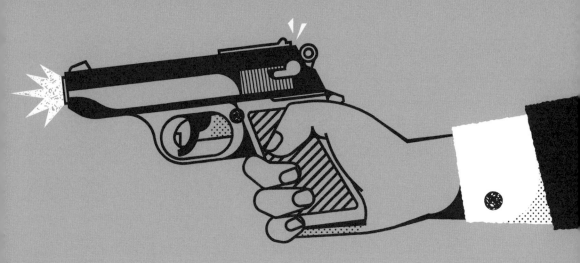

FIXED IT IN
POST-PRODUCTION

Before the advent of digital editing systems, filmmakers needed a lot more time to edit and put together the final cuts of their films, because the physical job of assembling a cut of a film took a lot longer.

Sometimes, they used this time to completely overhaul their work. In Ralph Rosenblum and Robert Karen's excellent book *When the Shooting Stops, the Cutting Begins: A Film Editor's Story*, Rosenblum explains just how much influence an editor can have over the final shape of a picture. He goes into great detail about how he effectively completely restructured William Friedkin's movie *The Night They Raided Minsky's* (1968) in his cutting room, being left pretty much to his own devices while Friedkin moved on to another project.

Fast forward to 2004, and a prequel was in the works to Friedkin's 1973 classic, *The Exorcist*. But from the footage shot, two films were spawned in post-production. Paul Schrader was the original director, but after a screening of his cut, the production company – Morgan Creek – panicked. It thus hired *Die Hard 2*'s director Renny Harlin to fix the film, and he shot numerous sequences, adding new characters and removing others. In the end, both versions were released, Harlin's as *Exorcist: The Beginning* in 2004 and Schrader's as *Dominion: Prequel to the Exorcist* in 2005. A rare insight into two different visions of what started as the same script, and how post-production choices shaped them.

In the digital era the post-production process can be completed in much less time. The same goes for distribution, too: gone are the days when heavy cans of film had to be duplicated and physically sent around the world. But there's been a consequence to this increased efficiency. Hollywood studios tend to want their films faster now, and digital editing and distribution facilitates that. The casualty is thinking time. *Mad Max: Fury Road* (2015) had three months built into the schedule just to watch all the footage, before a frame of it was edited. Conversely, some productions allow three months total to get the footage watched and a final cut put together. In an era where release dates can't be missed, this is probably why films are getting longer and longer: there just isn't as much time to shape them.

But post-production remains a pivotal phase – a period when decisions, ideas and last-minute changes can often affect a film dramatically. So, let's explore some of the on-screen moments that were decided long after filming on the movie was completed...

THE TICKING CLOCKS AND THE BLACKLIST

High Noon *1952*

A masterclass in how a film can be significantly enhanced by quality editing, *High Noon*, starring Gary Cooper, gradually amps up the tension by cutting to images of ticking clocks, giving the audience a constant reminder of the impending showdown.

The film was made as an allegory of the situation in Hollywood during the era of Senator Joseph McCarthy's infamous House Un-American Activities Committee, which investigated accusations of communism within Hollywood in the 1940s. The committee drew up a "blacklist" of filmmakers and performers who were believed to have communist ties, and these people were boycotted by the studios, finding it almost impossible to get work. Most tellingly, *High Noon* was a comment on how many people within the industry failed to stand up to the committee and stand up *for* those accused. This may have been

why the film didn't take the Best Picture Oscar that year, losing out to Cecil B DeMille's far safer *The Greatest Show on Earth* (1952).

High Noon doesn't play out in real time right down to the second, due to some tinkering after the first cut of the movie that slightly knocked things out. But it very nearly does, and every background clock is synced in time with where we are in the action. Legend also says that the ticking clocks that feature in the film weren't in the original cut. Apparently they were the work of editor Elmo Williams and director Fred Zinnemann, who introduced more shots of them to raise the tension throughout the film. This theory has been refuted by others, though, who insist that the clocks were there from day one.

Either way, a ticking clock has been used as a tension-raising device in many productions since then. The TV show *24* owes a significant debt to *High Noon* for one, and many films, including *Back to the Future Part III* (1990), have tipped their hat to the *High Noon* clocks.

FEWER INSTRUCTIONS

Fight Club *1999*

A small trim was made in the edit to *Fight Club* – bizarrely, at the request of the Los Angeles bomb squad. It's the sequence in the movie where the methodology for making TNT is being discussed. The DVD commentary for the film revealed that, after viewing the scene, the bomb squad asked for a few lines of the instructions to be removed.

DON'T CALL US

The Santa Clause *1994*

T he first run of prints of this festive family comedy starring Tim Allen that spawned a trilogy of movies contained a line in which Allen said: "1-800 SPANK-ME? I know that number." The problem? This number really did lead to "adult services" – a fact that came to light when a child dialled it after hearing it in the film. All versions since have had the line excised.

AN EDITING REVOLUTION

Don't Look Now *1973*

Nicolas Roeg's *Don't Look Now* expertly uses several storytelling techniques – foreshadowing for one (look at the frequent appearances of the funeral barge). But this was a film that also had a significant impact on the editing process thanks to Graeme Clifford, whose unusual editing choices dramatically enhanced the (already compelling) footage.

Clifford admitted that he deliberately cut some shots short, held others when there was little reason to, or suddenly cut to very different images. He wanted to throw people off balance and – unusually – to make the audience actively aware of the editing. Films as diverse as *Out of Sight* (1998), *Flatliners* (1990) and *In Bruges* (2008) are among the many influenced by the colour and editing choices in *Don't Look Now*.

DON'T SHOW, JUST TELL

Bambi *1942*

The irony of *Bambi's* most famous moment – the off-screen death of the young deer's mother – is that it was chosen as the softer option as the film neared its release. Originally, a sequence was discussed and drawn that would have shown the audience his mother dying in front of our eyes. But after some deliberation, it was decided that this was too intense for the intended family audience. That in some way, it'd be less traumatic not to show her death. The plan didn't work really, did it? While we'll never know if the alternative version would have left younger (and older) viewers as upset, there's a feeling that by letting imagination fill in the gaps, the mother's death was *more* upsetting. Although looking at the 1978 animated adaptation of *Watership Down* – where Hazel the rabbit dies before our eyes – it's not hard to see the counterargument...

THE COMPLETELY RETOOLED DISNEY FILM

The Emperor's New Groove *2002*

Almost all films go through sizeable changes throughout production, and the first draft of any film's script is usually quite different from the final version. But few films change as dramatically as *The Emperor's New Groove*. However, the comedy-heavy Disney production does occasionally show signs of what it originally was – a far more musically driven film that went by the name of *Kingdom of the Sun* and boasted a songbook by Sting.

When *Pocahontas* (1995) and *The Hunchback of Notre Dame* (1996) – both coming hot on the heels of one of Disney's best-ever runs – each fell short at the box office, the powers that be decided on a drastic change of course for *Kingdom of the Sun*, then in development. The plan for a music-heavy, environmentally themed film was all but jettisoned.

This process was fascinatingly documented in a film by Trudie Styler entitled *The Sweatbox* (2002), which was never officially released. The documentary tells of the project's about-turn, which eliminated almost all the songs but which did introduce the character of Kronk (shown above), who got his own spin-off straight-to-DVD sequel, helping to make the film more of a knockabout comedy than it had originally been. It's a good one, certainly, but the 40th in Disney's line of animated features was one of its toughest to realize behind the scenes.

A NOT-VERY-CLOSE SHAVE

Justice League *2017*
Mission: Impossible – Fallout *2018*

One of the most infamous stories of reshoots in the modern era comes from what was supposed to be the crowning glory of Warner Bros.'s collection of movies based on the DC Comics universe. The film *Justice League* went into production just weeks after *Batman v Superman: Dawn of Justice* (2016) – made by the same creative team – received middling to hostile reviews on its release, and Warner's top brass wanted to make sure this didn't happen again. Press were scrambled onto the set early in production to offer assurances that the studio had paid attention to feedback and was employing a lighter tone for its big mash-up that involved many DC heroes – Superman, Batman, Wonder Woman, Aquaman, the Flash and Cyborg.

But when Warner Bros. chiefs saw the first cut from director Zack Snyder, they clearly panicked. Joss Whedon – director of the first two *Avengers* movies – was persuaded to make the leap from Marvel to DC and come on board for rewrites, and substantial extra shooting was ordered. Which is what leads us to Henry Cavill's quite fascinating upper lip.

By the time Warner Bros. greenlit those reshoots (which Whedon rather than Snyder directed), Cavill was deep into production on a new project, *Mission: Impossible – Fallout*, for Paramount Pictures. Thing is, for his character in the *MI* movie, Cavill was sporting a moustache (see above), and when Warner asked Paramount if it would be possible to let our Henry have a shave, Paramount said no. The result is one of the most unusually off-putting examples of CG in modern cinema. In the early sequences of *Justice League*, Superman's lip appears to have a life of its own (you'd be forgiven for thinking it would emerge as a character in its own right, igniting memories of Richard E Grant's second head in *How to Get Ahead in Advertising*, 1989). In light of Paramount's refusal to cooperate, the decision was made to shoot the extra material with Cavill, and to get the visual effects team to remove the fur from his top lip. It's true to say that in this instance, their work was not subtle.

THE EXTRA ENDING

The Shawshank Redemption *1994*

Despite being destined to live its life in the top ten of the IMDb's "best films of all time", *The Shawshank Redemption* does find itself up against one regular criticism: its final scene. In fact there's a good reason why many people feel the film has a tacked-on ending. And that's because it has a tacked-on ending.

It's based on Stephen King's novella *Rita Hayworth and Shawshank Redemption*, and originally the movie was set to stop at the same point as the source material. This would have seen Morgan Freeman's Red, finally released from Shawshank, on a bus trip that may or may not reunite him with his best friend, Andy Dufresne. King deliberately kept his ending ambiguous – but studio executives weren't having any of it. They wanted closure. That's why in the film you hear Red's "I hope" voiceover as he gazes out the window of the bus, followed by a final scene in which that hope is realized, as Red and Andy reunite on the beach.

An extra point to watch for in *The Shawshank Redemption* comes earlier in the film, when you get to see a mugshot of a young Red. Turns out that picture isn't actually of a youthful Morgan Freeman – it's a picture of Freeman's son.

THE SEX SCENE WITH SOMEONE ELSE'S BODY

Supernova *2000*

At one stage, the forgettable sci-fi film *Supernova* was recut by *The Godfather* (1972) director Francis Ford Coppola in a bid by parent studio MGM to salvage something it liked. Original director Walter Hill was not impressed, and had his name taken off the credits. But the oddest reworking of a scene is an early moment of passion in the film.

Hill originally shot the scene with actors Peter Facinelli and Robin Tunney. It wasn't an easy sequence – a sex scene that theoretically takes place in a weightless environment. When Coppola was brought in to do the re-edit, he wanted to keep the scene, but he imagined it taking place between different characters. As such (and techniques to do this in the year 2000 were hardly advanced), the heads of Angela Bassett and James Spader were inserted, many months later, onto the twisting torsos of Tunney and Facinelli. The sex scene in the finished movie thus involves two characters, but the body parts of four different human beings.

BLURRY PLAYERS

Early Man *2018*

The climax of Aardman's charming stop-frame animation *Early Man* is a soccer match between characters from the Stone Age and the Bronze Age. It's a sequence that would be tricky to put together in any form of animation, but it was impractical to create it entirely in stop motion – a technique that requires physical models to be moved individually and painstakingly photographed one frame at a time.

Instead, director Nick Park deployed some digital animation work, carried out after the main body of filming was completed, to add the extra players in the background. But notice how they often appear slightly blurry and out of focus. There was a good reason for this: cost. The budget for *Early Man* was fairly modest, which meant that there wasn't the money to animate the extra players in huge detail.

That said, some change was spared in order to get the crowd noises just right. Hundreds of people gathered at the Bristol Rovers Football Club's stadium, where BBC TV show *The Choir's* host Gareth Malone supervised the crowds to record the chants.

MUSICAL MUPPET MISMATCH

Muppets Most Wanted *2014*
The Muppet Christmas Carol *1992*

The opening song of *Muppets Most Wanted* not only cheerfully shreds the credibility of sequels – "Everybody knows that the sequel's never quite as good" go the lyrics – but the song also finishes on the original title of the film rather than the one it ended up with. The felt ensemble sings, "It's the Muppets again" (set against a backdrop heavily influenced by old Busby Berkeley musicals, as shown above) and *The Muppets...Again!* was indeed the original moniker of the movie. Late in the day, however – too late for the song to be changed – Disney opted to rename the film *Muppets Most Wanted*. The filmmakers mulled over what to do about the lyrics but in the end they decided to leave them intact, simply cutting to a title card at the end of the song.

There's also a mismatch between the soundtrack album of Christmas favourite *The Muppet Christmas Carol* and the film now in distribution. "When Love Is Gone", which now plays over the end credits, was originally sung within the film itself by the character of Belle (Meredith Braun). Just prior to release, Disney's then-boss asked for it to be cut, believing that it wouldn't appeal to a younger audience. What muddles matters is that the scene reappeared in the original Laserdisc and VHS releases in 1993. An early DVD release also reincorporated the song, but subsequent versions have dropped it, or relegated it to a deleted scenes section. So, you are not alone if you recall seeing it but have wondered where it went. Did the scene ever exist? Yes, it absolutely did.

NEW SCORE, PLEASE

Chinatown, *1974*
2001: A Space Odyssey *1968*
The Graduate *1967*

Of the many extraordinary elements of *Chinatown*, the score by the late Jerry Goldsmith is a real standout. What makes it all the more remarkable is how quickly he turned it around. Phillip Lambro had composed and recorded what was supposed to be the score for the movie, but producer Robert Evans wasn't impressed – to the point where he rejected it outright. Goldsmith was drafted in and given just ten days to create a new score from composition to recording. It earned the composer an Oscar nomination, and came to be regarded as one of his finest pieces of work. No small feat.

Perhaps the most famous alternative-score story is that of *2001: A Space Odyssey*. Throughout the extensive production, director Stanley Kubrick (pictured above) used a selection of pieces by classical composers including Richard Strauss and György Ligeti to give him guidance. However, Hollywood composer Alex North had been asked to create an official score for the movie, which he duly did. He turned up at the film's première fully expecting to hear his work as the soundscape to

the film. But, of course, it wasn't. Nobody had told North, but during post-production, Kubrick had decided to stick with the classical pieces he'd been using all along. It wasn't until the 1990s that North's music for the film was finally released.

In the case of *The Graduate*, Paul Simon and Art Garfunkel were recruited to provide the songs. The problem was that they were incredibly busy at the time. They gave director Mike Nichols some of their existing work to use as a guide when putting the film together, with the intention of writing three fresh songs to add to this later on. But they never managed to fulfil this promise. Up against non-stop touring demands, ultimately the duo were only able to deliver one new song – a Paul Simon-penned number based (according to the film's director Mike Nichols) on the relationship between Joe DiMaggio and former First Lady Eleanor Roosevelt, in which Mrs Roosevelt became Mrs Robinson. The rest of *The Graduate*'s soundtrack remained existing numbers, although it's hard to imagine the film without them now.

CHANGE THE MUSIC

Grease *1978*

Producer Allan Carr had some very firm ideas of how to take *Grease* from stage to screen, wanting to change some of the story to reflect his own experiences of high school. When securing the rights, he managed to get a rare option to change or add music to the production. This resulted in some now-famous scenes being added that weren't in the stage show, including the sequence (shown above) right at the start that shows Danny and Sandy on a beach during the summer before the story begins. It's also why John Travolta gets to sing "Greased Lightnin'", a number that goes to a different character, Kenickie, in the stage show. Travolta was also the reason why so much original dialogue stayed intact. As Carr was writing the script, he began to veer away from the stage musical dialogue, but Travolta – who

had played Danny many times in the musical – kept drawing things back to their roots.

Take a look at the animation that begins the film and you'll see something that came together in a bit of a clunky way. In fact this sequence was created for a different song altogether – John D Wilson had animated the opening credits, but the music wasn't clicking. Barry Gibb of the Bee Gees was invited to come up with what would become the film's title tune, "Grease", which was added in post-production. But if you watch closely you'll notice that the lyrics are sometimes at odds with the animation. Despite objections that the song was too serious for the film that followed, it became a major part of the massively popular soundtrack album, selling 10 million copies in less than a year.

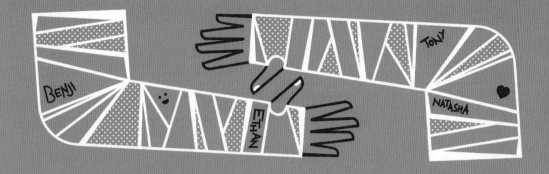

FIX MY ARMS!

Tag *2018*

Jeremy Renner managed to get through his *Mission: Impossible* and Marvel movies without coming to much harm, but an injury surprisingly befell him on the set of the rather tamer *Tag*. The comedy, which pretty much came and went at the box office, was hit by Renner breaking both his arms a few days into production. He was shooting a scene where he climbed up a stack of chairs, but as he did so, the rigging on them broke, flinging him to the floor and...well...ouch. For the rest of filming, he wore green plaster casts, which the post-production team removed using visual effects. Considering how often superhero characters are realized using post-production effects work, it's somewhat ironic that for Renner, those techniques were needed for what should have been a much more straightforward role.

WHAT TO DO WITH THOSE PUFFINS?

Star Wars: Episode VIII – The Last Jedi *2017*

Here's an example of a creative post-production trick in a movie that also generated a profitable merchandising line. For the filming of *Star Wars: Episode VIII*, the island of Skellig Michael off the coast of Ireland was used as Luke Skywalker's reclusive home. But the Jedi wasn't the only inhabitant; Skellig Michael is home to thousands of puffins, which were protected by a preservation order. As the film relied on a good chunk of filming on Skellig Michael, the puffins were regularly, unavoidably, in shot. What to do with them? Filmmakers decided to use the birds as placeholders for CG creatures – and behold, the Porgs were born.

CHANGING THE BOARDS

Die Hard With a Vengeance *1995*

I n this, the third *Die Hard* movie, the point where Bruce Willis's Detective John McClane meets his soon-to-be reluctant partner Zeus Carver (Samuel L Jackson) takes place after the former is forced by a terrorist to parade on the streets of New York City wearing a particularly offensive racist message on a sandwich board. This scene nearly caused the studio to drop the project, until backers threatened to shop the movie elsewhere (this is the only *Die Hard* movie not to have been overseen by 20th Century Fox, instead being produced by Cinergi and ultimately distributed by Touchstone).

The scene was shot on location in Harlem, and production got around the huge problems that would probably have surfaced had Willis worn the message for real by keeping it blank for the live shoot. Visual effects were used to add the offensive slogan afterward, and onlookers were none the wiser until the film was released.

In case you're interested, there's a rumour that *Die Hard With a Vengeance* screenwriter Jonathan Hensleigh was questioned by the FBI once his work was complete. Authorities were concerned by how much he knew about the storage of federal gold in New York City. They were assuaged when he revealed his source to be a *New York Times* article.

STRANGE VOICES

Hercules in New York *1970*
Greystoke: The Legend of Tarzan, Lord of the Apes *1984*
Despicable Me 2 *2013*

If you think that Arnold Schwarzenegger doesn't sound very Schwarzenegger-y in his Hollywood debut, *Hercules in New York*, you're not mistaken. The production company feared that Arnie's accent was too thick, and brought in someone else to dub his lines. Shortly afterward, said production company went bankrupt – a fact that kept the film off the shelves for years.

A similar fate befell Andie MacDowell when making *Greystoke: The Legend of Tarzan, Lord of the Apes*. This was director Hugh Hudson's first film since he was Oscar-nominated for *Chariots of Fire* (1981), and there were high expectations for it. The film had problems, though, and MacDowell's accent was deemed to be one of them. Her southern tones were thought not to suit the part, so the voice you hear is actually that of Glenn Close.

For really late redubbing, though, the mere days that the team behind *Despicable Me 2* had to rework a character in their film is worthy of note. The character of antagonist Eduardo Perez (in red, above) was meant to have been voiced by Al Pacino, but just a month before release – with his lines recorded and the character animated – Pacino left the project, reportedly due to creative differences. Benjamin Bratt was brought in, but there was no time to rework the animations, so he spent five days in a recording booth working hard to match the existing voice movements. It's testament to Bratt's skill that you can barely notice the change.

THE CORRECTED STARFIELD

Titanic *1997*

Updating and reissuing films as special editions got something of a bad name when George Lucas started tinkering with his *Star Wars* films. But sometimes a rerelease allows a filmmaker to correct a blink-and-you'll-miss-it error.

That was the case when James Cameron's *Titanic* was being prepared for its 3D cinema rerelease in 2012. Cameron took the opportunity to change the background of a certain shot, because of a comment made by astronomer Neil deGrasse Tyson after the original film's release. It related to the point in the film where Kate Winslet's character, Rose, is seen staring up at the stars. Tyson had noted that the pattern of stars in the sky shown doesn't match what she would have seen at that location and at that point in time. Cameron, a renowned perfectionist, investigated the matter and discovered Tyson was right. He got the astronomer to send over the correct starfield – and that's what you see in every copy of the movie put out since then.

UNUSED IN ONE FILM, USED IN ANOTHER

Blade Runner *1982*
The Shining *1980*

Now that director Ridley Scott has decided that *The Final Cut* (2007) – rather than the *Director's Cut* (1992) – is, well, the final version of sci-fi masterpiece *Blade Runner*, the opening voiceover that plagued the original cinema release is slowly being consigned to history. Scott never wanted it, and nor did anyone who saw any other cut of the film. It was added at the insistence of the studio Warner Bros., who also wanted a happy ending.

Scott had the job of cobbling together footage to satisfy the studio's demands. And in order to achieve this, the director looked beyond his own movie. The sequence at the end of the film in the original cinema cut, with aerial shots of the countryside intercut with Harrison Ford's Deckard and Sean Young's Rachael driving away, wasn't filmed for *Blade Runner* at all. Instead, they're shots that Stanley Kubrick filmed for the long drive to the Overlook Hotel in *The Shining*. In typical Kubrick fashion, though, he had an awful lot of footage that wasn't used, and he told Scott to help himself to it for the new – and widely disliked – ending to *Blade Runner*. This ending has been jettisoned in every subsequent cut.

TONE IT DOWN

O Brother, Where Art Thou? *2000*
Saving Private Ryan *1998*

The Coen brothers' delightful comedy *O Brother, Where Art Thou?* (shown right) was a significant, if barely noticed, moment in cinema technology. Joel and Ethan Coen wanted their film to have a warm, sepia glow and a period feel. One reason for this was to offset the fact that the locations for filming were often very green, which wasn't the look the brothers wanted. As a result of this, it became the first film to use a full digital colour-correction system to alter the colour palette.

For *Saving Private Ryan* (shown right), director Steven Spielberg wanted less colour saturation in his shots, to give the movie a raw, rough look. To achieve this, he didn't use protected lenses while filming, which gave the footage a gritty, unpolished feel. He also ensured that the brightness was toned down and the colour desaturated in post-production.

NEW DIRECTOR, PLEASE

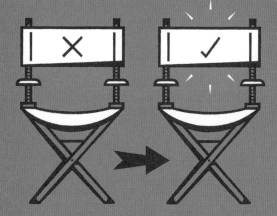

Geostorm, *2017*
Fierce Creatures *1997*
Jaws 2 *1978*

Sometimes, when a film requires extensive post-production work and reshoots, the original director can't or won't be involved.

One example is *Geostorm*. Original director Dean Devlin didn't oversee the final cut of the movie, nor the $15 million of reshoots that were ordered by producer Jerry Bruckheimer (who was brought on to the project after poor test screenings). That job went to Danny Cannon, who took charge of the new characters who were added to the film very late in the day.

When the decision was made in post-production to change the ending of *Fierce Creatures*, the problem was simply one of scheduling. The comedy is most notable for reuniting the award-winning cast of *A Fish Called Wanda* (1988), but after test audiences were unimpressed with the original denouement, a new one was planned. Problem: Michael Palin was in the middle of filming a BBC documentary series around the Pacific Ocean, which would eat up much of his year. The production had no option but to wait for his return and delay the release. That, in turn, meant that director Robert Young couldn't film the new material, so Fred Schepisi stepped in to oversee the new ending instead.

In the case of *Jaws 2*, director John D Hancock was simply replaced after the first month of his footage was reviewed. Hancock's take on the *Jaws* sequel was far darker than the forgettable final version that was released. His film would have focused on – and don't forget this was actually shot – an Amity Island in swift decline, on the verge of going out of business after the events of the first movie. But this was never a story that the studio was particularly comfortable with. To add to the on-set troubles, the residents of Martha's Vineyard, where the film was shot, were reluctant to board up their windows to give the impression of an area going bust. Hancock was replaced, the film hastily retooled and Jeannot Szwarc came in as director – but only after Steven Spielberg turned down the offer.

CAMEOS, APPEARANCES AND CROSSOVERS

When Tom Cruise took on a rare supporting role in Paul Thomas Anderson's Oscar-nominated *Magnolia* (1999), its UK distributor designed its poster to give the then-biggest movie star in the world top billing. That he was one part of an ensemble was no matter: said distributor wanted to sell tickets, and thus it was determined to use Cruise's name, in spite of the US promotional campaign being far lower key.

Perhaps, then, this is why Paramount would treat Cruise's surprise appearance in 2008's *Tropic Thunder* as such a closely guarded secret. It certainly worked. Buried under heavy prosthetics, Cruise played tasteless movie studio boss Les Grossman, and the secret was intact come the film's opening weekend. His scene-stealing performance gave the film a huge word-of-mouth boost, and that first tranche of audiences a genuine surprise.

It's hard to think of a better way to use such a cameo role. Edgar Wright has certainly very much bought into that way of thinking. His triumphant comedy hit *Hot Fuzz* (2007) is a cauldron of surprise appearances and crossovers (as are several of his films). As well as being part of the loosely connected "Cornetto" trilogy and thus linked to the other films in the DVD collection, *Shaun of the Dead* (2004) and *The World's End* (2013) – see "There Are Signs", page 29 – the list of cameos ranges all the way from Wright and Simon Pegg's mothers to *The Lord of the Rings* director Peter Jackson. Wright is such a cine-literate filmmaker that his movies drip with love for the medium and the people within it, in the form of frequent salutations and references.

Wright isn't alone, either. There's something quite special about a film that organically, and unexpectedly, manages to overlap with another. That, or the surprise appearance of someone you're not expecting that actually enhances the film in question. Sure, some cameos and appearances are clearly for the headlines – hello David Beckham in Guy Ritchie's *King Arthur: Legend of the Sword* (2017) – but others have a slightly less cynical reason behind them.

Throughout this chapter, then, we're going to look at those unexpected appearances of particular performers and characters in productions, as well as exploring a few of cinema's more unusual (and not always official or intended) crossovers. As always, heed the spoiler warning at the start of the book (page 7).

THE UNIVERSES THAT FOLDED

The Mummy *2017*
The Amazing Spider-Man 2 *2014*
Spider-Man: Homecoming *2017*
Venom *2018*

The 2017 movie reboot of *The Mummy* was not greatly loved, earning poor reviews and disappointing box-office takings. Tom Cruise headlined the film, but one of the most uncomfortable performances in it was Russell Crowe as Dr Henry Jekyll. And this wasn't a cameo, which could be easily dismissed, either. Ahead of the release of *The Mummy*, Universal announced that it was introducing its own cinematic world of horror films (including remakes of many of the studio's classics), by the name of the Dark Universe. *The Mummy* was to be the first official entry in the series, and the character of Dr Jekyll was there to set up future storylines. A cast picture featuring Crowe, Cruise, Johnny Depp, Javier Bardem and Sofia Boutella was released as a teaser of some of the new universe's ensemble. Only three of them appeared in *The Mummy*, and the critical backlash to the film led Universal to back away from more Dark Universe movies.

This wasn't the only time a cinematic universe was seeded in a big film only to be abandoned subsequently. Sony was keen to mimic the success that Marvel was enjoying with its cinematic universe, peopled by the likes of Iron Man and Captain America. As holder of the screen rights to the character Spider-Man, Sony wove into *The Amazing Spider-Man 2* a blatant set-up for a future Sinister Six movie, which would have brought several key Spider-Man foes together in one production.

Drew Goddard had signed up to write and direct *Sinister Six* for Sony (which meant forsaking the director's chair on 2015's *The Martian* – a job that went to Ridley Scott), and the six villains are overtly referenced at the end of *The Amazing Spider-Man 2*. The problem was that while the film did solid business, it failed to commercially improve on its predecessor. Against growing fan backlash over unremarkable *Amazing Spider-Man* films, Sony temporarily abandoned its spinoff universe. A couple of years later, though, Sony inked a deal with Marvel that led to the sharing of the Spider-Man character between Sony and the Marvel Cinematic Universe. And when *Spider-Man: Homecoming* (2017) proved a more successful venture, Sony had fresh confidence in its spin-off universe and, as a result, it decided to greenlight *Venom*, starring Tom Hardy.

CLOSE-UP TIME

Sunset Boulevard *1950*

Legendary Hollywood producer Cecil B DeMille adds gravitas to *Sunset Boulevard* by cameoing as...legendary Hollywood producer Cecil B DeMille. In the scene in question, fading Hollywood star Norma Desmond assumes that DeMille has invited her to the studio to discuss a screenplay she'd been working on. No such invitation was forthcoming and, as it turns out, she was invited to the studio by an executive who simply wanted to rent her car.

Director Billy Wilder was keen to land DeMille for the cameo, and it was something of a coup to achieve this. And not a cheap one. DeMille charged $10,000 for his appearance, plus a new Cadillac. When Wilder wanted him back to get a close-up, DeMille billed the production another $10,000. Inflation adjusted – roughly $200,000 minus the car – that ain't bad for a bit of work.

WHERE IS THAT?

Commando *1985*
Predator *1987*
Die Hard 2 *1990*

They may not be linked by an overt cinematic universe, but there's a small bond that ties together this trio of action hits. It is the fictional Central or South American nation of Val Verde, created by writer Steven E de Souza to avoid the political or diplomatic difficulties that might arise if the events were set in a real place.

Val Verde was first name-checked in Arnold Schwarzenegger-headlined *Commando*. It was then worked into the script of *Predator* and, a few years later, in *Die Hard 2*, when viewers learned that the villainous General Ramon Esperanza is flying into Washington's Dulles Airport. Where's he coming from? You've guessed it. It's a small touch, of course, but one that links three otherwise disparate films.

SILVER STORM

Who Framed Roger Rabbit *1988*
Grand Canyon *1991*

One of many challenges director Robert Zemeckis faced when putting together his ground-breaking live-action and animation hybrid *Who Framed Roger Rabbit* was finding someone to play a yelling director right at the start of the movie. Zemeckis wanted a screaming, fretting filmmaker to blast Roger for fumbling his lines, in the style of then-notorious producer Joel Silver (pictured above left), who had earned a reputation for his short temper on movies such as *Lethal Weapon* (1987) and *Predator* (1987). In the end, somebody had a simple idea: why not just ask Joel Silver? As such, Silver took on his only live-action speaking role in a movie to date.

Silver may have proved the inspiration for another character, too. In the ensemble drama *Grand Canyon* (cast pictured above right), Steve Martin plays a producer called Davis who trades in blood-and-guts movies. It's widely believed that writer–director Lawrence Kasdan based Davis on him. *Grand Canyon* is also notable for having one of the most out-of-nowhere moments of violence in an otherwise tonally calm drama. The film primarily comprises middle-aged, middle-class characters having conversations, but there's a vicious bolt from the blue when Martin's movie producer gets shot in the leg while being mugged.

A FAMILIAR TALE

Goodfellas *1990*
My Blue Heaven *1990*

Goodfellas and the generally forgotten Nora Ephron-penned comedy *My Blue Heaven*, starring Steve Martin and Rick Moranis, are based on the same story. Watch them back to back and you'll see that Ray Liotta and Steve Martin are both playing real-life gangster Henry Hill (called Vinnie Antonelli in *My Blue Heaven*). In fact, you could argue that *My Blue Heaven* is an indirect sequel to *Goodfellas*, as – in spite of being made first – it picks up the story of Henry Hill from just about where *Goodfellas* leaves him.

IT'S YOU AGAIN

Jackie Brown *1997*
Out of Sight *1998*

Michael Keaton didn't take on many acting roles in the 1990s, but he did play the same character twice, a year apart. *Jackie Brown* and *Out of Sight* were made by different studios (Miramax and Universal) – which straight away tends to make legalities rather complex, given that rival studios are rarely keen to share characters – but Keaton played FBI agent Ray Nicolette in both productions. The link between the films, of course, is that they were both based on novels by Elmore Leonard.

AUTHORS SNEAKING INTO THE BACKGROUND

Wonder *2017*
Yes Man *2008*
The Exorcist *1973*
Deliverance *1972*
Creepshow *1982*
Pet Sematary *1989*

For the finale of *Wonder*, based on the novel by R J Palacio, an end-of-term prizegiving scene brings together the parents and children in the story. Prominently sitting behind Julia Roberts is Palacio herself (pictured below right). As it happened, once the footage was in the can, the filmmakers ran through the sequence again, but instead read a tribute to Palacio by way of both surprising the author and thanking her.

Authors cameoing in film adaptions of their own works is nothing new, of course. Some don't get lines, such as when Danny Wallace appears in the background of a bar scene in the film take on *Yes Man*. William Peter Blatty's cameo in *The Exorcist* (shown opposite, top left) is more pointed. Blatty penned the original book, and went toe to toe several times with

director William Friedkin on the direction of it. He was given a small part in the movie, playing a film producer, where there's an argument over the inclusion of a particular scene. There's an in-joke here, of course, given that these were just the kind of arguments that Blatty and Friedkin were engaged in.

Author James Dickey wasn't a particularly welcome presence on the set of *Deliverance*, the film based on his novel. The story goes that the author turned up on set and got into a heated, alcohol-fuelled exchange with director John Boorman, who had co-written the screenplay of Dickey's novel. The exchange got physical, although Boorman and Dickey soon made amends. To keep Dickey involved, but away from the writing, Boorman offered him a small role as Sheriff Bullard (above, top right) in the movie. Dickey initially declined the offer before later returning to film the scene.

But it's Stephen King who is, well, the king of cameos. Look out for his appearances as a man covered in green plants all the way back in the original *Creepshow* and as a priest conducting a funeral service in the 1989 version of *Pet Sematary* (above, left and right).

PLAYING AGAINST TYPE

It's a Mad, Mad, Mad, Mad World *1963*

Stanley Kramer's ambitious, star-packed comedy *It's a Mad, Mad, Mad, Mad World* has a terrific – albeit brief – moment where we see the Three Stooges (shown above). The trio's reputation as outstanding physical comedy performers is superbly played against, too. In a movie where everyone else seems to be moving around and causing trouble, the three of them are seen standing in a line, looking miserable.

THE UNNAMED CROSSOVER

Collateral *2004*
The Transporter *2002*

For a brief moment in Michael Mann's *Collateral*, Tom Cruise's Vincent finds himself at an airport, trading cases with an unnamed courier played by Jason Statham. It's widely assumed that the character is Frank Martin, who Statham played in *The Transporter*. The reason the character couldn't be named is likely because the films were from different studios and it may have caused legal issues.

SURPRISE STAN LEE APPEARANCES

Avengers: Endgame *2019*
Mallrats *1995*
Teen Titans Go! To the Movies *2018*

The king of the comic-book movie cameo was the late, great Stan Lee (shown above), who had a small role in every single movie set in the Marvel Cinematic Universe up to and including the fourth Avengers film, *Avengers: Endgame,* which was released in 2019, the year after Lee's death. And in fact his extensive lists of cameos would have been even longer had his brief scenes in the movies *Blade* (1998) and *Kick-Ass* (2010) not been edited out in post-production.

It was filmmaker Kevin Smith who first had the idea of a Stan Lee cameo. Smith, a huge fan of Lee (the creative force behind Marvel comics) and a devoted comic-book fan, wrote a role for Lee in his second movie, *Mallrats*. That role was Lee playing himself, who we first meet signing books at the shopping mall where the film is set. Lee then returns later in the film to pass on some life and love tips to Silent Bob.

Lee only had one cameo in a movie based on a property for Marvel rival DC Comics. That was 2018's delightful *Teen Titans Go! To the Movies*, where he lends his voice to a joke about how he's turned up in the wrong film.

PASSING THE TORCH

The Rundown *2003*

TOO OLD FOR THIS SHIT

Maverick *1994*
Lethal Weapon series *1987–98*

A small but pivotal moment in action cinema can be seen in the comedy *The Rundown* (known in the UK as *Welcome to the Jungle*), an early vehicle for Dwayne "The Rock" Johnson who was being positioned as the next big thing in action cinema. Meanwhile, Arnold Schwarzenegger's action career was in decline, as he set off down a political path. He makes a cameo appearance in *The Rundown*, walking out of a nightclub as Johnson's character walks in, seemingly passing the torch with the words "Have fun". Johnson certainly does, as his character goes on to cause mayhem...

T he jocular style of 1994's comedy western *Maverick* (based on the 1950s TV series of the same name, and with James Garner as one of its leads) had the team behind the *Lethal Weapon* franchise at its heart: Mel Gibson in front of the camera and director Richard Donner behind it. That's why you get a lovely moment where Gibson's Maverick finds himself in the middle of a bank robbery. The man behind the mask? That'd be Danny Glover. The pair eye each other up before Glover utters the line "I'm too old for this shit" – his trademark in the *Lethal Weapon* movies.

THEY AIN'T PRETENDING

Interstellar *2014*

The opening interviews for Christopher Nolan's sci-fi hit *Interstellar*, where elderly people talk about living through a natural disaster, set the scene for the film to follow. They establish that Earth is in peril, nearing the end of its days, thanks to the ravages of climate change.

However, with the exception of one interview, none of the people recalling their experiences at the start of the film was filmed for *Interstellar*. In fact, they're talking about a real-life environmental disaster: Nolan and his team licensed material from the 2012 documentary mini-series *The Dust Bowl* by acclaimed filmmaker Ken Burns, which explored a period during the 1930s when drought and dust storms struck the Great Plains of America, having a devastating impact on agriculture and the inhabitants. The only actor in that opening sequence is Ellen Burstyn, and hers is the only scripted interview. The rest are real people talking about their experiences of a disaster that took place 100 years or so before *Interstellar* is set, with significant poignancy.

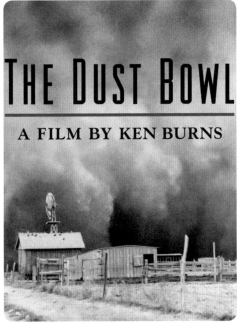

A QUESTION OF SPELLING

Manhunter *1986*
The Silence of the Lambs *1990*
Hannibal *2001*
Red Dragon *2002*
Hannibal Rising *2007*

While the majority of films based on Thomas Harris's character Hannibal Lecter have been linked by the casting of Anthony Hopkins (below right) in the role, his wasn't the first portrayal of the cannibalistic killer on the big screen. Brian Cox (right) got there first in 1986, in Michael Mann's *Manhunter*, which was based on the novel *Red Dragon*. In this movie the character is Dr Hannibal Lecktor – for reasons unknown, the spelling of the name was changed from the source.

Manhunter's box-office disappointment paved the way for director Jonathan Demme to bring a different interpretation of Lecter to the screen, in 1990's *The Silence of the Lambs*, which saw Hopkins's brilliant debut. More than a decade later he reprised the role in *Hannibal*, and for his third run at it, in the film *Red Dragon* he found himself headlining a very different take on the book in this prequel to the two previous films. But that wasn't the last we saw of Lecter – a further production, *Hannibal Rising*, was an origin story that saw Gaspard Ulliel take on the iconic role.

THE QUIET CINEMATIC UNIVERSE

Sixteen Candles *1984*
The Breakfast Club *1985*
Weird Science *1985*
Ferris Bueller's Day Off *1986*
Dogma *1999*

Although there are no direct links between them, director John Hughes regularly set his now-iconic films of the 1980s in the same fictional location. This was the town of Shermer, Illinois, which was based on Hughes's own hometown of Northbrook, Illinois. Shermer High School is a key setting in films such as *Sixteen Candles*, *The Breakfast Club*, *Weird Science* and *Ferris Bueller's Day Off*.

Shermer pops up in another film, too. Kevin Smith's controversial *Dogma* is notable for being a movie that Smith himself helped fuel protests against when it sparked religious complaints; he stood on the picket lines alongside protesters who were oblivious to who he was (the subsequent publicity boost was dramatic). The movie includes the characters Jay and Silent Bob, who appear in many of Smith's films (as well as making a surprise cameo in 2000's *Scream 3*). In the case of *Dogma*, they're on a pilgrimage to Shermer in homage to the Hughes films they watched in their youth.

WATCH OUT FOR TOURISTS

The Lady Vanishes *1938 and 1979*
Night Train to Munich *1940*
Millions Like Us *1943*
Crook's Tour *1941*
I See a Dark Stranger *1946*

For Alfred Hitchcock's 1938 film *The Lady Vanishes* (pictured top right), a pair of characters were introduced into the script to give a little comic relief. The characters were conceived by screenwriters Frank Launder and Sidney Gilliat, and they went by the names of Charters and Caldicott, played respectively by Basil Radford and Naunton Wayne.

This pair of chattering tourists were introduced as cricket fans, keen to get home for the test match. But Launder and Gilliat liked their creations, and set about reusing them in further productions. Thus, the pair popped up in 1940's *Night Train to Munich* (pictured middle right) and 1943's *Millions Like Us*, before being spun out into their own BBC radio productions. There was even a film of those radio adventures under the title *Crook's Tour* (pictured bottom right).

The fun came to an end in 1946, with *I See a Dark Stranger*. By this time, actors Wayne and

Radford wanted the roles beefed up. Launder and Gilliat refused, and the fallout meant that the actors were stopped from playing characters with those names again.

That said, the characters were revived in 1979 by British horror firm Hammer Film Productions for its remake of *The Lady Vanishes*. This time, Arthur Lowe and Ian Carmichael took on the roles. A BBC television series, again recast, would follow in the 1980s. Entitled *Charters and Caldicott*, it starred Robin Bailey and Michael Aldridge, and ran for just six episodes.

THE SAME GANGSTER

The Cotton Club *1984*
Hoodlum *1997*

American gangster Ellsworth "Bumpy" Johnson was facing federal charges when he died of heart failure in 1968, at the age of 62. He's been brought to the screen a few times, but Laurence Fishburne has played him twice, in slightly different ways and under different character names. The first time was in Francis Ford Coppola's *The Cotton Club* (above left), where the character's name was changed to "Bumpy" Rhodes, but was clearly based on Johnson. Move forward to 1997, when Bill Duke's film *Hoodlum* (above right) brought Johnson's story overtly to the screen with Fishburne in the lead role.

THANKS FOR THE MUSIC

Wayne's World *1992*
Bohemian Rhapsody *2018*

The moment in *Wayne's World* where Wayne and Garth (Mike Myers and Dana Carvey) sing Queen's hit "Bohemian Rhapsody" in the car had a real impact on the band's exposure in America. While the band had enjoyed success in the States, guitarist Brian May credited this sequence with reigniting their fame there. So, when it came to shooting the biopic of Queen frontman Freddie Mercury, *Bohemian Rhapsody*, a role was found for Mike Myers. He plays a brash music studio executive who tells the Queen band members that "no one is going to be head-banging in the car to 'Bohemian Rhapsody'".

IS THAT YOU, MR BOND?

The Cannonball Run *1981*
Goldfinger *1964*
For Your Eyes Only *1981*
Inspector Gadget *1999*

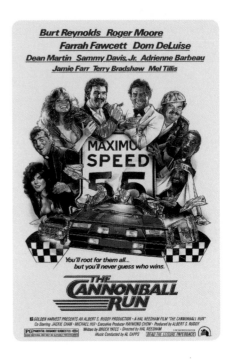

For some time, there were rumours that the producers of the James Bond films – Eon Productions – were considering legal action against the makers of *The Cannonball Run* for the number of 007 references in the movie. In fact, director Hal Needham would subsequently meet with Eon over the possibility of helming a Bond movie (he never did), and the issue was apparently brought up at that meeting!

The first obvious crossover is the fact that Roger Moore stars in it. He also drives an Aston Martin DB5 – a car made famous when Sean Connery drove it as 007 in *Goldfinger*. The car is fitted with gadgets too, not least an ejector seat.

Mostly, though, the character Moore plays, Seymour Goldfarb, Jr., is pretty much James

Bond. Although the name of 007 is never mentioned, eyebrows were still raised, especially as *For Your Eyes Only*, Moore's fifth James Bond movie, premiered just days after *The Cannonball Run* was released. The legal threat was sidestepped, incidentally, when Roger Moore promised Bond producer Albert R Broccoli that he would never do anything to hurt the character of 007.

A Richard Kiel aside: it's worth zipping to the end of 1999's forgettable *Inspector Gadget* movie to note a delightful cameo from Jaws – the character played by the late Richard Kiel in *The Spy Who Loved Me* and *Moonraker* in the 1970s – along with other familiar foes. That scene (for which Kiel is credited as the "Famous Bad Guy with Silver Teeth") attracted less legal interest.

A TRIBUTE IN RETURN

Land of the Dead *2005*
Paul *2011*

The scene (shown above) in George A Romero's belated sequel *Land of the Dead* where a group of well-to-do people have their photos taken next to chained zombies features a pair of well-known faces. Each taking credit as "Photo Booth Zombie" are Simon Pegg and Edgar Wright. Romero gave them the cameos after being thoroughly impressed with their loving tribute to his work in their own film, *Shaun of the Dead* (2004).

Another affectionate tribute (albeit with a foul-mouthed alien at the heart of it), comes in the form of science-fiction comedy *Paul*, written by and starring Simon Pegg and Nick Frost. This tribute is to the works of Steven Spielberg and includes overt nods to *Close Encounters of the Third Kind* (1977) and *E.T. the Extra-Terrestrial* (1982). As an added bonus the eponymous alien character (voiced by Seth Rogen) puts a call through to Spielberg to give him advice about the making of *E.T.*, specifically suggesting that the creature's finger should glow. The voice on the other end of the phone really is Spielberg, too – a nice touch that was actually the veteran director's idea. He knew Pegg from making *The Adventures of Tintin* (a film that was also released in 2011, but which had been in production much longer), and when he heard about *Paul* he asked if he could do the vocal cameo in the movie. And who says no to Spielberg?

DIRECTORS IN MOVIES

Jay and Silent Bob Strike Back *2001*
Good Will Hunting *1997*
Austin Powers in Goldmember *2002*
Wes Craven's New Nightmare *1994*
The Wrong Man *1956*

I t's not just actors that enjoy popping up unexpectedly in films (see page 200). Directors also like making the odd cameo.

Kevin Smith's comedy, *Jay and Silent Bob Strike Back*, features Ben Affleck and Matt Damon. The pair had won an Oscar a few years previously for co-writing *Good Will Hunting*, in which they both starred. That film was directed by Gus Van Sant, and there's a lovely comedy sequence in Smith's film in which Van Sant, playing himself, is seen counting the easy box-office loot from that film as he mulls a possible sequel.

"Sir" Steven Spielberg happily pulls his own leg in a cameo in *Austin Powers in Goldmember*, where he appears alongside other famous faces seen to be remaking the Austin Powers story for the big screen. As Austin guides him on how to make the scene work, Spielberg drops in that he's won an Academy Award.

Wes Craven becomes a key character in his reinvention of the *A Nightmare on Elm Street* series, *Wes Craven's New Nightmare*. The film, which paved the way for the *Scream* franchise and its postmodern, self-deprecating approach to horror cinema, sees Craven – who directed the original *A Nightmare on Elm Street* (1984) as well as this film – troubled by his creation and wanting to make a new film in order to end Freddy Krueger once and for all. Spoiler: this film did not end Freddy Krueger once and for all.

It would be remiss not to mention Alfred Hitchcock and the many cameos he made in his own movies. But he went a step further for *The Wrong Man* (shown opposite; see if you can spot him in the background), a film loosely based on a true story. He introduced the film with a speech directed at the audience, filmed in a very shadowy, Hitchcock-like way, explaining that unlike his previous thrillers, this one is very much grounded in real life.

A FEW LAST THINGS....

Director Robert Zemeckis has admitted that there's a problem with his films. How should they be categorized? Video shops of old – and Netflix menus of late – want to slot a film easily into a certain genre; they want it to be categorically a comedy, a thriller, a sci-fi film… But not everything fits comfortably. Just because the video shops of old, and the streaming services of now, want to fit everything into a certain place, it doesn't necessarily mean that the movies themselves are always willing to play ball.

And if you were the author of a book that's packing in lots of movie secrets which were, on the whole, neatly categorized, what would you do with the ones that weren't? Or the little tales that just about struggled to find their place elsewhere, but were still very much worth talking about?

The answer, clearly, is to bundle together the ones that don't fit elsewhere into a lovingly crafted section at the end of the book. Which is what brings us all here. Did you know, for instance, that satellites in the cruelly overlooked *Geostorm* (2017) were named in part after other Gerard Butler movies? That around a third of 1985's *Rocky IV* is made up of flashbacks and montages, and the film is all the better for it? That one of the reported reasons that Neo wears such a long coat in *The Matrix* (1999) is that it made it easier for the special effects and animation teams? And that Jim Henson had to crouch out of sight for the best part of two days, to capture the shot where Kermit the Frog sings "Rainbow Connection" in the middle of a swamp at the start of *The Muppet Movie* (1979)?

Heck, were you also aware that the *Home Alone* franchise was inspired by a moment in 1989's *Uncle Buck*, where a pre-stardom Macaulay Culkin is seen peeking through his character's home's letterbox? Might just win you a pub quiz, that.

This, then, is the Zemeckis chapter – the place where you'll find the awkward stories that don't neatly fit elsewhere but that still deserve their turn in the spotlight. One last time, then, here we go…

YOU CAN CLEAN THAT UP...

THE REDFORD CROSSOVER

Drop Dead Fred *1991*

Three Days of the Condor *1975*
Sneakers *1992*

In a memorable scene from *Drop Dead Fred*, Rik Mayall walks across a clean carpet with dog poo on the bottom of his shoe. To begin with Mayall went method, smearing dog mess onto his shoes for the first take, giving the set a particular aroma. For later takes, he used a mix of chocolate cake and peanut butter. Director Ate de Jong later commented: "We used take three, but I still smell take one when I see it."

There's a lovely similarity between two very different thrillers made at two very different times. In *Three Days of the Condor*, the character of Joseph, played by Robert Redford, manages to avoid arrest by nipping out to get a sandwich. In a moment that's hardly likely to be coincidence, in 1992's *Sneakers* Redford's character, Martin Bishop, avoids the same fate – this time by popping out for pizza.

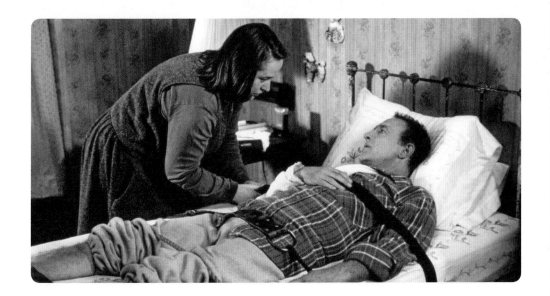

IN SEQUENCE

Boyz N the Hood *1991*
Misery *1990*

Most of the time, movies are filmed out of sequence due to the demands of different locations and the assorted personnel in the cast and crew, as well as factors that are out of reasonable control. But some films have been shot in sequence, by and large – a process that can have a subtle impact on the end result.

John Singleton's astonishing movie debut, *Boyz N the Hood*, is one such production. The decision was made mainly because of Singleton's inexperience: he had never directed before and didn't really know how to, so his producer Steve Nicolaides scheduled the movie shoot in sequence to help him. Singleton says that doing it this way helped him learn as he went along, and claims that you can see how he improves toward the end of the film, where he took more chances.

In Rob Reiner's film adaptation of Stephen King's novel *Misery* (shown above), it wasn't inexperience but rather intensity that led filmmakers to schedule the drama pretty much in sequence.

The bulk of the movie is set in the home of Annie Wilkes (Kathy Bates), as she tends to James Caan's Paul Sheldon after a car accident. While the few exterior parts of the film were scheduled as normal, most of it was shot in sequence on a set. As such, Reiner had Caan lie in bed for around three months as filming progressed, in line with what his character was experiencing. The tension that developed between the two lead characters – and Caan and Bates also reportedly clashed on set – is palpable, especially going into the final act of the story.

THE REAL DRAWINGS

Pocahontas *1995*

Glen Keane is one of the most famed Disney animators of his generation, bringing to life the Beast in *Beauty and the Beast* (1991) and Ariel in *The Little Mermaid* (1989), among others. But Keane has noted that you don't get to see any artist's pure work in an animated feature. By the time a picture makes it to the screen it has been redrawn, coloured and touched up to the point where it has essentially become the work of several people.

Yet there's one exception to that. *Pocahontas* (pictured above) is the only film in which some of Keane's work appears completely unaltered. These are the raw drawings, done using charcoal, that appear during the film's central musical number, "Colors of the Wind". While most of the song is fully touched up animation as usual, we get – deliberately – to see rougher drawings as part of the sequence.

Keane created the drawings using a computer, but intentionally kept the charcoal lines in, without a clean-up artist coming in to take the rough edges out, as would normally happen on an animated feature (with initial drawings gradually worked up to become the finished, fully rounded visuals that you usually see). It remains the only time in Keane's extensive Disney career that this happened.

THE PLOT HOLE THAT STUMPED FILMMAKERS

Ocean's Eleven *2001*

Ask a screenwriter on any heist movie and they'll say that one of the biggest challenges is making sure the logic of the crime holds up on screen – that an awful lot of time is spent working out whether the whole thing is plausible. One heist movie that took some liberties in that regard is the 2001 remake of *Ocean's Eleven*, with an ensemble cast led by George Clooney as the character Danny Ocean.

To begin with we're expected to believe that three casinos some distance apart in Las Vegas would share one big underground vault. But we can forgive that. What's harder to overlook is a plot hole that filmmakers only discovered after the film had wrapped – too late to fix it.

The final part of the plan, which allows the crew to get away with a haul of $160 million, sees a bag switch take place in the vault, after which the bags are carried out to waiting security vans before Ocean and his crew return, disguised as a SWAT team. It's these bags that are tracked and intercepted at the airport – only to discover that they're full of fliers.

The question is, as director Steven Soderbergh acknowledged on the film's DVD commentary, how did those bags get into the vault in the first place? They're too big to have been snuck down there. The filmmakers admitted afterward that they had no plausible explanation for the plot hole. Best just go with it, eh?

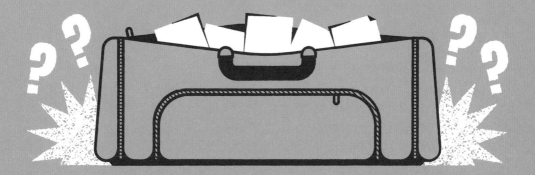

WHAT CANE?

Willy Wonka & the Chocolate Factory *1971*

The first time Gene Wilder appears as Willy Wonka (above), in the 1971 adaptation of Roald Dahl's book, *Charlie and the Chocolate Factory*, we see him walking with a limp and carrying a cane for support. It's a far cry from the extrovert character that the audience was expecting based on the build-up earlier in the film. In fact, the unexpected style of his entrance was a condition Wilder himself imposed before he would accept the role. In a letter to director Mel Stuart, the actor explained that he wanted his Wonka to initially be seen as physically restricted, before his cane hits the cobblestones and he stands up and launches into a somersault. His intention was that "from that time on, no one will know if I'm lying or telling the truth".

METHOD

In the Name of the Father *1993*

Daniel Day-Lewis is renowned for the lengths he'll go to to bring truth to a role. None more so than in *In the Name of the Father*. The acclaimed film recounts the true story of the Guildford Four (the four men wrongly convicted of the 1974 Guildford pub bombings in the UK) and zeroes in on Day-Lewis as Gerry Conlon. Ahead of the scene in which an exhausted, scared Conlon signs a confession, the actor was locked up for three days and nights in a prison cell, interrogated every nine hours and kept awake throughout the night by people banging on the door and throwing water over him. By the time he arrived on set, Day-Lewis's appearance and emotional state were exactly what was needed to bring force to his performance.

AVOIDING A RATING

Annie *1982*
Robin Hood: Prince of Thieves *1991*
Snakes on a Plane *2006*

A lot of stories surrounding ratings are about the lengths filmmakers have gone to in order to reduce their ratings certificate to a 12A or PG-13 (awarded respectively by the BBFC in the UK and the MPAA in the US), which allow the broadest possible audience to see a movie.

U and G ratings invite a broader crowd in theory, but some filmmakers worry that such ratings are off-putting to teenagers and to others who (wrongly) assume that these only apply to kids' films. This has led some studios to take steps to *increase* the ratings of their films. The film adaptation of the musical *Annie* was one such example. The filmmakers added two lines – "Come back here, you goddamned kid!" and "God dammit!" – just to make sure it would be given a PG rating rather than a G in America (PG-13 would follow as an option later in the 1980s).

Christian Slater improvised an expletive on the set of *Robin Hood: Prince of Thieves*, uttering the line, "fuck me, he cleared it". This had to be cut from the UK release to get a PG certificate, but many thought that the line inoculated the movie from a too-soft G rating in the States.

In the case of *Snakes on a Plane*, the Samuel L Jackson-headlined internet (rather than box-office) phenomenon actually had its toilet sex scene added, to ensure an R rating in America. Before that, distributors were afraid that it would be classified PG-13, which they deemed way too soft for the kind of film they were making.

GAINED IN TRANSLATION

Despicable Me *2010–ongoing*

There's a universal appeal to the scene-stealing Minions (shown above) in the *Despicable Me* movies, which has earned them their own films (both long and short). Virtually every Minion you see on-screen is voiced by the same person – co-director Pierre Coffin, who has spent extensive periods in the recording booth to nail the Minions' dialogue. Listen closely, though, and you'll notice that there's more to the Minions' apparent gibberish than first appears. In fact, Coffin is blending different languages from across the planet to form the Minions' speech. Thus, you'll get flavours of English, French, Spanish, Italian and Japanese, for instance.

THE ODD LINE

Coyote Ugly *2000*

A solid hit in 2000, *Coyote Ugly* was – as is the case with many biggish Hollywood productions – the product of lots of screenwriters' input. Among those hired to do a rewrite of the script was Kevin Smith, riding high on his successes with *Clerks* (1994) and *Dogma* (1999). But Smith gave a rare insight into the rewrite process when he revealed that in spite of being paid a hefty sum, only one line of his can be heard in the movie. The words "I'm not a lesbian, I played in the minors, but never went pro" probably cost the studio at least five figures. Ironically, given Smith's extensive comic-book background, the fact that the lead character is a comic-book fan had nothing to do with him.

THE SWEARIEST SCENE TO GET A FAMILY-FRIENDLY RATING

The King's Speech *2010*

Colin Firth's expletive-laden monologue in the Academy Award-winning *The King's Speech* includes a good dozen f-bombs, as the future King George VI struggles to overcome his stammer. What's unusual about the core scene with the future king and his speech therapist Lionel Logue, in which he utters a tirade of explosive language, is how lenient movie censors were toward it. The British Board of Film Classification (BBFC) might allow a smattering of lighter swear words in a 12A movie, but it usually enforces a strict one-f-word-only rule for that certificate, allowing children younger than 12 to watch if accompanied by an adult.

The board made a rare exception for this scene in *The King's Speech*, noting that the movie "contains strong language in a speech therapy context". It was a sizeable box-office hit in the UK and overseas. But concerns remained in America about the level of swearing, so for the US market, a separate version of the film was later released that cut out the more profane language. That version promptly bombed at the box office. The original cut? It went on to win Best Picture at the Oscars, while Firth walked away with Best Actor.

PAINFUL STEPS

Dirty Dancing *1987*

Patrick Swayze and Jennifer Grey's climactic performance in *Dirty Dancing* (above) is one of the best-loved scenes of the 1980s. But what's not obvious is how much pain Swayze was in. He had a problem knee, exacerbated by his Broadway schedule before he began work on the film, and throughout the production had to apply ice to temper the swelling. In particular, the scene in which Johnny and Baby practise their routine on a log compounded his injury. In fact, Swayze had barely any cartilage left in his knee. As he recalled in his memoir, he was left with bone grinding on bone. The pain was intense – and would be throughout each dance sequence.

KEEP IT SHORT

Frankenstein *1931*

A small bit of post-production censorship helped create an iconic line in *Frankenstein*, from director James Whale. The full line that Dr Frankenstein was set to utter was: "It's alive! It's alive! In the name of God. Now I know what it feels like to be God!" But this fell foul of the censors at the time, who felt that the religious references could cause offence. That's why some earlier versions of the film truncated the line to "It's alive! It's alive!", although later re-releases have restored the full speech.

DEATH OF A CAT STROKER

For Your Eyes Only *1981*

If the makers of Roger Moore's third James Bond adventure were looking for impact with the opening of the movie, they sure got it. Legendary cat-loving Bond nemesis Ernst Stavro Blofeld is seen nearly killing 007 by sabotaging his helicopter in the pre-credits sequence. Bond then exerts his revenge by picking up Blofeld's wheelchair with his helicopter, and dropping him down a gigantic chimney. Blofeld, it seems, is dead.

Or is he? Watch again, and you'll notice that no one mentions Blofeld's name. That wasn't for story reasons, though. At the time, the Bond series was engaged in a legal battle with *Thunderball* (1965) co-writer Kevin McClory

who was developing his "unofficial" remake of *Thunderball* (which became the 1983 film *Never Say Never Again*) and who claimed the rights to the character of Blofeld. (*Never Say Never Again* is one of only two James Bond films not made by Eon Productions – the original *Casino Royale*, 1967, being the other – and is not considered part of the 007 cannon.)

Producers of *For Your Eyes Only* deliberately didn't name Blofeld in that opening sequence in order to avoid getting sued. But the ambiguity that this created over the identity of the man in the wheelchair also gave them a handy getout for bringing Blofeld back in future Bond adventures.

DO AS YOU'RE TOLD

To Live and Die In L.A.   *1985*

On the director's commentary for the disc release of *To Live and Die In L.A.*, William Friedkin revealed how he nearly hit problems when filming a chase scene in Los Angeles airport. He'd gained permission to do so from officials, but this came with a collection of caveats due to the fact that the actors would have to run through a working airport.

Real-life patrons of the airport couldn't be filmed, so extras would be needed. Then, for part of the chase, Friedkin was told that lead actor William Petersen wouldn't be allowed to get up and run along the dividers that separated the moving sidewalks in the terminal building.

Friedkin ignored the sidewalk rule, and Petersen did the scene as required. This put the director on the receiving end of heavy chastisement from those very airport officials who'd given him permission in the first place. But after an angry rebuke, he was allowed to use the footage in the film.

ALL THE LINES

All the President's Men *1976*

Dustin Hoffman and Robert Redford (pictured above, left to right) were determined to make their conversations – with their now-famous interruptions – in *All the President's Men* feel authentic. As such, the pair took the unusual step of memorizing not only their own dialogue, but also each other's. Knowing perfectly what was coming allowed them to intervene convincingly, and be utterly in the right place in the script. It gave their interactions a brilliantly natural ebb and flow.

SPARE CHANGE

The Matrix Reloaded *2003*

The first sequel to *The Matrix* (1999) is generally regarded as a disappointment, but it does have some standout moments. One of them is the long Agent Smith fight sequence, where Keanu Reeves's Neo fights against a sizeable number of Agent Smiths, played by Hugo Weaving. It's evident just from watching it that the logistics are staggering. However, so was the cost. This sequence is believed to be the most expensive ever filmed, with the bill running into tens of millions of dollars.

HELPFUL MILITARY

Godzilla *2014*

It's a cliché of Hollywood disaster movies that when the military swoop in to help, they make things worse. But for his take on *Godzilla*, director Gareth Edwards wanted to turn that cliché on its head and show a more realistic side to military intervention (albeit in an unrealistic situation!). Edwards brought in a military advisor from the Pentagon to keep things on track, and when it came to David Strathairn's Admiral Stenz (above), they took a more human approach to his decision-making. So instead of calling for an attack, this admiral looks for peaceful solutions, opting for a visual pursuit of the title critter, rather than reaching for guns and missiles.

CAMERON EFFECT

Escape from New York *1981*

He may be known for directing, but you can also see James Cameron's craft in John Carpenter's *Escape from New York*. Cameron was the special effects director of photography and responsible for one particularly special effect – creating a matte version of New York City for a scene showing a wireframe zoom-in from the perspective of a glider. It looks digital, but it's not at all. The cost of doing it that way at the time would have been prohibitive, so instead Cameron made a set of New York from black-painted models and reflective white sticky tape. A camera was then flown through this miniature set to make it look like a digital reading of the city.

CLOSING IN

12 Angry Men *1957*

Keep your eye on the style of the shots Sidney Lumet deploys in his classic *12 Angry Men*. As we are introduced to the jurors, locked in a room deliberating a case, Lumet uses wide shots. As the film progresses, however, and the tension mounts up, Lumet and cinematographer Boris Kaufman gradually edge the camera. By the end of the film, the jurors are shown in sharp close-up, with Lumet looking to inject real claustrophobia into the drama.

Note, too, that this is a film where character names are never given save for an exchange at the end of the picture where two of them finally reveal theirs. Leaving them unnamed was a deliberate device – these men could stand for anyone; it could be any one of us in that jury room.

PLAY THAT TUNE

Big *1988*

The sequence in *Big* (above) in which Tom Hanks and Robert Loggia play the tune "Heart and Soul" by jumping on the keys of a floor piano is one of the best-loved parts of the movie this side of the Zoltar machine. The keyboard was a fixture in the FAO Schwarz toy store on Fifth Avenue, New York City (which closed in 2015), but while plenty of fans went there to mimic the performance, they weren't quite getting the real McCoy. The movie needed a bigger piano than the one at the store in order to accommodate the two actors. It *is* Hanks and Loggia performing the scene, though, although doubles were on set the day they shot the sequence in case they fumbled their moves. They didn't. Other things that didn't exist when the movie was made include the Zoltar machine, but look closely and one can be seen in the background of *Step Up 3D* (2010).

HOW MUCH?

Shallow Grave *1994*

The total budget for Danny Boyle's debut feature *Shallow Grave* came to just over £1 million. Coincidentally, the film hinges on its main characters discovering a million pounds in banknotes. The money needed to be seen, but this wasn't simply a job for the props department – Boyle wanted the readies to look real (plus, the Bank of England has strict rules about faking its notes), so he decided to use genuine banknotes. Where, then, could the filmmakers get the cash? Simple. They hired it. In exchange for £1,000 of the film's budget, Boyle and his team were given £1 million in cash for a 24-hour period. Thankfully, every pound of the million was returned safely, with no penalty. Good job too, given that the production eventually had to auction off its own props in order to see the movie through to completion.

SINGIN' IN THE RAIN

For such a universally loved mix of comedy and musical, *Singin' in the Rain* (1952) was an unhappy production, for a number of reasons.

1 Donald O'Connor was given a solo number by Gene Kelly, who was keen for his co-star to have a song of his own. This evolved into the "Make 'Em Laugh" song and dance routine, which included O'Connor doing a somersault off the wall, among other exertions. Although only in his twenties, O'Connor was a heavy smoker, and after shooting the scene was confined to bed for a week through exhaustion. When he returned to the set it was only to discover that the camera equipment had failed so he had to shoot the whole scene again.

2 Watch Kelly sing and dance his way through the incredible title number sequence, and you'd never guess that he was suffering from a heavy fever on the day.

3 The dubbing sequence sees Debbie Reynolds's character Kathy overdubbing the voice of Jean Hagen's Lina Lamont. But there's more going on than meets the eye. The film would have us believe that Reynolds is dubbing Hagen, but the truth is that Hagen sang the song herself, just at a lower pitch. Yep: Hagen dubbed Reynolds dubbing Hagen.

4 Kelly was a famously hard worker, and expected the same of his cast. His drive pushed Reynolds, who was just 19 years old, to tears. It took a pep talk from Fred Astaire – who was shooting a movie next door – to give her the confidence to go back out and deliver her terrific performance. Reynolds was later quoted as saying that the toughest things she ever did in her life were making *Singin' in the Rain* and giving birth.

5 The song "Singin' in the Rain" wasn't written for the film and had appeared in movies before, most notably being sung by Judy Garland in *Little Nellie Kelly* (1940). Only two songs in the final movie were written for it, one of which nearly caused legal problems. "Make 'Em Laugh" is very similar to Cole Porter's "Be a Clown". Legendary songwriter Irving Berlin reportedly visited the set and noted this similarity himself. The subject was swiftly changed and no legal challenge was ever made.

6 Kelly made the film partly because it was set at the MGM studio, to which he was contracted at the time. Following the film's success, and after being sometimes very awkward and tricky during the production, Kelly was finally able to negotiate his exit from the contract, agreeing to make three further films for MGM before it was cancelled.

REFERENCES

All websites accessed February 2019

CLUES, HAT TIPS AND HIDDEN DETAILS

Totems, p17 www.youtube.com/watch?v=Ms56y
WZak9w

What's in the Logo?, p18 www.reddit.com/r/
harrypotter/comments/37uakl/spoilerless_notice_
how_in_all_the_intros_of_the/

What's Cap Been Missing?, p20 https://marvel
cinematicuniverse.fandom.com/wiki/Captain_
America%27s_To-Do_List

Watch Your Meds, p22 www.reddit.com/r/movies/
comments/2u2fhz/the_secret_joke_in_silence_of_
the_lambs/

The Clue Is in the Score, p24 https://twitter.com/
filmeastereggsstatus/1020913564293349376?lang
=en

WORKING AROUND PRODUCTION CHALLENGES

Introduction, p33 https://www.denofgeek.com/
movies/23335/hart-bochner-interview-ellis-in-die-
hard-directing-and-more

Late Redubs and Cuts, p34 *21 Jump Street* DVD
commentary track, Sony Pictures International,
2012

Clint Moves Fast, p35 www.youtube.com/watch?
v=cuT0Cfu-j5o

Quiet Breakthroughs, p36 www.newyorker.com/
tech/annals-of-technology/how-michael-crichtons-
westworld-pioneered-modern-special-effects

The Yankees Fan in the Mets Hat, p38 Crystal,
Billy, *Still Foolin' 'Em*, London: Virgin Books, 2015

Tom's Nose, p39 www.ted.com/talks/j_j_abrams
_mystery_box/discussion?nolanguage=en%2F%2F
www.xpertar.com%2Fhollywood%2F2016%2F11

A Bit of Bed Rest, p42 Goodwin, Cliff, *Sid James:
A Biography*, London: Arrow Books, 1996

The Injured Movie Star, p44 Armstrong, Vic, *The
True Adventures of the World's Greatest Stuntman*,
London: Titan Books, 2012

A Familiar Dance, p48 www.youtube.com/watch?
v=uM13nF6JScA

Cary's Nudge, p49 www.youtube.com/watch?v=
sweYws_hh0g

Get Off My Lawn!, p49 www.reddit.com/r/Movie
Details/comments/9c6nf6/in_friday_1995_a_
resident_in_the_neighborhood/

Matching Twins, p50 www.youtube.com/watch?v=
BHRygj6fgmE

Hero in a Tight Space, p51 *Batman Returns* Blu-
ray director's commentary, Warner Bros., 2018

More Pain, p52 Reynolds, Burt, *But Enough About
Me*, London: Blink Publishing, 2015

The Late Post-Credits Sequence, p54 www.denof
geek.com/movies/don-hall/don-hall-interview-big-
hero-6-and-his-most-bizarre-screening

Practical Ingenuity, p55 https://twitter.com/vashi
koo/status/1040093692583763968?lang=en-gb

DETAILS, CHOICES AND MOMENTS

Empty Frames, p61 Higgins, Colin, *Harold and
Maude*, Chicago: Chicago Review Press, 2015

Who Needs Actors?, p64 *One Flew Over the
Cuckoo's Nest* DVD commentary track, Warner
Home Video, 1999

The Passage of Time, p67 Rubin, Danny, *How to
Write Groundhog Day* (Kindle Edition), Gainesville:
Triad Publishing Company, 2012

Beware Translations..., p68 www.reddit.com/r/
MovieDetails/comments/85la1b/in_anchorman_
veronica_eats_at_escupimos_en_su/
Debuting as James Bond, p70 Moore, Roger, *The
007 Diaries: Filming Live and Let Die*, Stroud: The
History Press, 2018
The 30-Seconds-a-Year Shot, p71 Salamon, Julie,
The Devil's Candy, London: Jonathan Cape, 1992
Where's Fact, Where's Fiction?, p72 Parker, Tom,
Jack Nicholson – The Biography, London: John Blake,
2017
The Joke Everyone Seemed to Miss, p76 *The
Naked Gun: From the Files of Police Squad!* DVD
commentary, Paramount Home Entertainment UK,
2001

ON-SET MOMENTS
The Arguments Behind a Comedy Classic, p87
Dworkin, Susan, *Making Tootsie (Film Study)*, New
York: Newmarket Press, 2011
Surprise!, p91 Mottram, James and David S Cohen,
Die Hard: The Ultimate Visual History, London: Titan
Books, 2018
Dancing through the Air, p92 www.youtube.com/
watch?v=CNSHjZmvZTM
Mirror Image, p95 *Sunset Boulevard* DVD extras,
Paramount, 2003
What the Actors Couldn't See, p96 www.den
ofgeek.com/movies/pride/31945/andrew-scott-
interview-pride-sherlock-statham
 The Illusion in a Movie Ending, p99 *Field of
Dreams* DVD, "Making of..." documentary, Universal
Pictures Video, 2003
Change of Character, p102 Eliot, Marc, *Steve
McQueen*, New York: Three Rivers Press, 2012
Scenes Shot on the Quiet, p104 Galloway,
Stephen, *Leading Lady: Sherry Lansing and the
Making of a Hollywood Groundbreaker*, New York:
Three Rivers Press, 2018

RAMIFICATIONS AND INSPIRATIONS
A Silver Lining, p113 www.upf.edu/pcstacademy/_
docs/200411_environment1.pdf
I Now Pronounce You..., p115 https://ew.com/
movies/2018/08/18/winona-ryder-keanu-reeves-
married-dracula/
Get Me More Scrat, p118 www.denofgeek.com/
uk/movies/ice-age/41955/the-ice-age-movies-and-
the-story-of-scrat
When Arnie Channelled a Legend, p119
Schwarzenegger, Arnold, *Total Recall*, Simon &
Schuster, 2012
Opportune Casting, p120
www.reddit.com/r/MovieDetails/comments/989b51/
this_wolverine_easter_egg_in_the_opening_credits/
The Coen Brothers' Way, p121 Tarantino,
Quentin, *True Romance: The Screenplay*, Berkeley:
Avalon Travel Publishing, 2000
The Groundbreaking Use of Technology, p123
Dawson, Nick, *Being Hal Ashby: Life of a Hollywood
Rebel*, Lexington: University Press of Kentucky, 2011
Frogs and the Bible, p126 www.filmdetail.
com/2008/01/12/8-and-2-in-magnolia/
**Moments that Changed Modern Product
Placement, p127** Hamsher, Jane, *Killer Instinct:
How Two young Producers Took on Hollywood*, New
York: Broadway Books, 2003
Eerily Close to the Truth, p129 *The Conversation*
DVD commentary track, Studiocanal, 2011

HOMAGES, MOTIFS AND CROSS-REFERENCES
Symmetry, p134 http://vimeo.com/kogonada/videos
Religious Metaphors, p136 http://www.mtv.com/
news/2436200/paul-verhoeven-robocop-christ-
story-remake-update/
The Classic that Inspired a Blockbuster, p143
"Shot by Shot", article in *Premiere* magazine, June
1996
Frames Per Second, p144 www.upress.state.ms.
us/books/423

Long Takes, p146 www.independent.co.uk/
arts-entertainment/films/features/guillermo-
del-toro-interview-the-shape-of-water-oscars-
mimic-weinstein-miramax-pans-labyrinth-
harvey-a8197751.html

SETS AND LOCATIONS
A Different Game, p154 https://insidethemagic.
net/2018/02/interview-wreck-ralph-2-directors-
rich-moore-phil-johnston-discuss-disney-
princesses-jokes-fate-unlucky-bunny/
Destroyed After Use, p156 Aiello, Danny, *I Only
Know Who I Am When I Am Somebody Else: My Life
on the Street, on the Stage, and in the Movies*, New
York: Gallery Books, 2015
The Mystery of the Lost Painting, p161 www.
bbc.co.uk/news/av/entertainment-arts-30467820/
lost-painting-auctioned-after-discovery-in-stuart-
little-film
Spielberg's Take on the Future, p164 www.denof
geek.com/movies/15773/alex-mcdowell-interview-
designing-minority-report
The Location that Helped Make the Film, p166
The Truman Show DVD extras, Paramount Home
Entertainment, 2006
Skyfall, p172 www.spyculture.com/dept-energy-
climate-change-documents-skyfall/

FIXED IT IN POST-PRODUCTION
Introduction, p175 Rosenblum, Ralph and Robert
Karen, *When the Shooting Stops, the Cutting Begins:
A Film Editor's Story*, Cambridge, MA: DaCapo Press,
1986
Fewer Instructions, p177 *Fight Club* DVD
commentary, Twentieth Century Fox, 2004
An Editing Revolution, p178 www.criterion.com/
current/posts/3466-editing-don-t-look-now
Blurry Players, p183 www.denofgeek.com/uk/
movies/nick-park/54736/nick-park-interview-early-
man-aardman-the-wrong-trousers-the-beano

Musical Muppet Mismatch, p184 www.denof
geek.com/movies/muppets-most-wanted/29884/
james-bobin-interview-muppets-alice-2-statham
Change the Music, p186 Hofler, Robert, *Party
Animals: A Hollywood Tale of Sex, Drugs, and Rock
'n' Roll Starring the Fabulous Allan Carr* (Kindle
Edition), Cambridge, MA: DaCapo Press, 2010
Fix My Arms!, p187 www.indiewire.com/2018/
06/jeremy-renner-broken-arms-tag-story-
interview-1201971936/

CAMEOS, APPEARANCES AND CROSSOVERS
Authors Sneaking into the Background, p200
Palacio, R J, *Wonder: Now a Major Motion Picture*,
Knopf Books for Young Readers; Movie Tie-in
edition, 2017

A FEW LAST THINGS…
You Can Clean That Up…, p216 https://twitter.
com/ate_jong/status/1061547454666076160
The Real Drawings, p218 www.denofgeek.
com/movies/16686/disney-legend-glen-keane-
interview-tangled-computer-animation-his-heart-
attack-and-ollie-johnston
What Cane?, p220 www.lettersofnote.com/2012/
06/part-of-this-world-part-of-another.html
Gained in Translation, p222 www.hollywood
reporter.com/behind-screen/despicable-me-2-
minions-5-579907
**The Sweariest Scene to Get a Family-friendly
Rating, p223** www.bbfc.co.uk/releases/kings-
speech-film
Painful Steps, p224 Swayze, Patrick and Lisa
Niemi, *The Time of My Life*, London: Simon &
Schuster, 2010
Do As You're Told, p226 *To Live and Die In L.A.*
DVD director's commentary, Twentieth Century
Fox, 2004
How Much?, p230 *Shallow Grave* DVD
commentary, MGM, 2001

PICTURE CREDITS

All stills are the copyright of the respective film studios and distribution companies. Every attempt has been made to credit these. We apologise if any omissions have been made.

23a Columbia Pictures; 95 Paramount Pictures; 205 PBS; **Alamy Stock Photo** 11a Everett Collection/20th Century Fox; 11b TCD/Prod.DB/Dreamworks; 12 Moviestore Collection/A24; 15 AF Archive/Touchstone Pictures/Buena Vista Pictures; 16 Moviestore CollectionWarner Bros; 19 AF Archive/Columbia Pictures; 21bl Pictorial Press Ltd/Paramount Pictures; 21br World History Archive/Goskino; 24 AF Archive/Paramount/Warner Bros; 27a Everett Collection/Paramount Pictures; 27b PictureLux/The Hollywood Archive/Warner Bros; 31 PictureLux/The Hollywood Archive/Paramount Pictures; 37b Granger Historical Picture Archive/Radio Pictures; 38 Everett Collection/Columbia Pictures; 41bl AF Archive/Rank Film Distributors; 41br Entertainment Pictures/Rank Film Distributors; 42 Pictorial Press Ltd/Rank Organisation/American International Pictures; 47a TCD/Prod.DB/20th Century Fox; 49 Moviestore Collection/Metro-Goldwyn-Mayer; 51 AF Archive/Warner Bros; 53a Lifestyle Pictures/Paramount Pictures; 53b Collection Christophel/Universal Pictures; 54a BFA/Marvel Studios/Walt Disney Studios Motion Pictures; 54b Everett Collection/ Walt Disney Studios Motion Pictures; 59 Photo 12/United Artists; 64 United Archives GmbH; 66 Pictorial Press Ltd/Walt Disney Studios Motion Pictures; 70 AF Archive/United Artists; 74 TCD/Prod.DB/Paramount Pictures; 76a & bl Photo 12/Paramount Pictures; 77l Pictorial Press Ltd/Compass International Pictures/Aquarius Releasing; 77r AF Archive/Paramount; 78 Lifestyle Pictures/ Universal Pictures; 79 Everett Collection/United Artists; 81 Pictorial Press Ltd/Warner Bros; 84 PictureLux/The Hollywood Archive/ Columbia Pictures; 87 TCD/Prod.DB/Columbia Pictures; 90 TCD/Prod.DB/MGM/UA Entertainment Co; 97 Everett Collection Inc/ Paramount Pictures; 98 Photo 12/20th Century Fox; 101 Everett Collection Inc/United Artists; 105l ScreenProd/Photononstop/ Universal Pictures; 115 Pictorial Press Ltd/Columbia Pictures; 116 United Archives GmbH/20th Century Fox; 119l AF Archive/TriStar Pictures; 121 Entertainment Pictures/Circle Films; 122l AF Archive/Warner Bros; 122r Aurora Photos; 124 PictureLux /The Hollywood Archive/Continental Distributing; 133b AF archive/Buena Vista Pictures/Walt Disney Pictures/Pixar Animation Studios; 134a AF Archive/Fox Searchlight Pictures; 134b BFA/Fox Searchlight Pictures; 139l Photo 12/United Artists; 141b Eddie Gerald/20th Century Fox; 141a Everett Collection/Toho; 143 TCD/Prod.DB/Metro-Goldwyn-Mayer; 144 AF Archive/Golden Princess Film Production; 145 TCD/Prod.DB/American International Pictures; 151a AF Archive/Paramount Pictures; 151b Everett Collection/United Artists; 154 TCD/Prod.DB/Universal Pictures; 157 Lukasz Janyst/20th Century Fox; 159a AF Archive/20th Century Fox; 161TCD/Prod.DB/ Sony Pictures Releasing; 163b AF Archive/Cinema International Corporation/Orion Pictures/Warner Bros; 163a AF Archive/ITC Entertainment & RAI; 164 Moviestore Collection/DreamWorks Pictures; 166 AF Archive/Paramount Pictures; 168r AF Archive/ Universal Pictures; 171 AF Archive/Warner Bros; 176 Entertainment Pictures/United Artists; 179 AF Archive/Buena Vista Pictures; 180 Everett Collection/Paramount Pictures; 183 Collection Christophel/StudioCanal; 184 Moviestore Collection/Walt Disney Studios Motion Pictures; 186 PictureLux/The Hollywood Archive/Paramount Pictures; 189 PictureLux/The Hollywood Archive/Universal Pictures; 192a Everett Collection/Buena Vista Pictures; 192b Pictorial Press Ltd/Paramount Pictures/DreamWorks Pictures; 198r Everett Collection/20th Century Fox; 200 Lifestyle Pictures/Lionsgate Films; 201ar & bl Everett Collection/Warner Bros; 201br TCD/ Prod.DB/Paramount Pictures; 202 Everett Collection/Universal Artists; 203l Collection Christophel/Columbia Pictures Industries; 203r Everett Collection/Gramercy Pictures; 205a A F Archive/Paramount Pictures; 206a A F Archive/Warner Brothers; 206b Photo 12/Archives du 7e Art/Orion Pictures Corporation; 208b Everett Collection/Anglo American; 209l Entertainment Pictures/Zoetrope Studios; 209r Moviestore Collection/United Artists; 210 Everett Collection/20th Century Fox; 211 United Archives GmbH; 213 PictureLux/The Hollywood Archive/Warner Bros; 217 TCD/Prod.DB/Castle Rock Entertainment; 218 AF Archive/Walt Disney Studios Motion Pictures; 220 AF Archive/Warner Bros; 222 Everett Collection/Universal Pictures; 224 AF Archive/Great American Films Limited Partnership; 227 Collection Christophel/Warner Bros; 228 PictureLux/The Hollywood Archive/Warner Bros; 229b Everett Collection/United Artists; 229bc Impress Movie TV/United Artists; 229ac Moviestore Collection/United Artists; 230 AF Archive/20th Century Fox; **Getty Images** 63a Steve Schapiro/Columbia Pictures; 73 Ron Galella Collection; 85 ullstein bild/Pathé Exchange; 105r Sunset Boulevard/Universal Pictures; 146 John Kobal Foundation/Paramount Pictures; 185 Jean-Philippe Charbonnier/Metro-Goldwyn-Mayer; 198l Ron Galella, Ltd/WireImage; 201al Steve Schapiro/Corbis via Getty Images; **REX Shutterstock** 37a Kobal/ Paramount Pictures; 45 Kobal/Hawk Productions/Columbia Pictures; 47b Kobal/Paramount Pictures; 92a, b & c Robert Quirk/Kobal/ Metro-Goldwyn-Mayer; 119r Kobal/Metro-Goldwyn-Mayer; 133a Toho; 137 Kobal/Warner Bros; 139r Kobal/Metro-Goldwyn-Mayer; 149 Kobal/United Artists; 159b Snap/Warner Bros; 168l; 173 Danjaq/Eon Productions/Kobal/Sony Pictures Releasing; 208a Kobal/ Gainsborough; 229a Kobal/United Artists; **Ronald Grant Archive** 63b Columbia Pictures; 208 Metro-Goldwyn-Mayer/20th Century Fox; **TopFoto** 23b Ullstein Bild/Universal International.

INDEX

Page numbers in italics refer to pictures and photographs

A

Absence of Malice   140
The Abyss   111
An Affair to Remember   72
Air Force One   160
Aladdin   111
Alien   46, 47, *47*, 88, 136, 158, *159*
All the President's Men   128, 227, *227*
The American President   169
American Sniper   35
Anchorman: The Legend of Ron Burgundy   68
The Apartment   139, *139*
Arthur   142
The Artist   153
Avatar   81
The Avengers   54, *54*, 180, 203
The Aviator   100

B

Back to the Future   28, 30, 132, 176
Badlands   121
Bambi   178
Batman   51, *51*, 83, 103, 158, *159*, 180

Battle Beyond the Stars   133
Battleship Potemkin   21, *21*
Beauty and the Beast   48, 58, 111, 218
Being There   26, 123
Big   230, *230*
Big Hero   6 54, *54*
The Birds   46, 47
Black Swan   95
BlacKkKlansman   114, 132
Blade   203
Blade Runner   153, 191
Blood Simple   121, *121*
Blow Out   145
Bohemian Rhapsody   209
Boléro   111
The Bonfire of the Vanities   71
Bound for Glory   123
The Bourne Identity   104
Boyz N the Hood   217
Bram Stoker's Dracula   115, *115*
Brazil   155, 156
Breakfast at Tiffany's   153
Brief Encounter   93
Broken Arrow   144, 169
A Bug's Life   133, *133*

C

The Cannonball Run   210, *210*
Captain America   20

Carrie   145
Carry On...   42, *42*, 158, 159
Casablanca   27, *27*
Casino Royale   225
Cast Away   11, *11*
Chariots of Fire   116, *116*, 189
Chinatown   33, 185
City Heat   52, 53
City Lights   59, *59*
City Slickers   38, *38*
Cleopatra   158, 159
Close Encounters of the Third Kind   117, 211
Clue   26, *27*
Coming to America   125, 140
Cool Hand Luke   136, 137, *137*
"Cornetto Trilogy"   29
The Cotton Club   209
Coyote Ugly   222
Creepshow   200, 201
Crook's Tour   208, *208*

D

Dance Dance Revolution   20
Dark City   158
The Dark Knight   83, 172
Das Boot   46
The Day After Tomorrow   113
The Dead Zone   12
Deadpool   138
Deep Blue Sea   109

Deliverance 200, 201, *201*

Despicable Me 148, 189, *189*, 222, *222*

Dick Tracy 15, *15*

Die Hard 33, 91, 175, 188, 197

Dirty Dancing 224, *224*

Dirty Harry 46

Do the Right Thing 154, *154*

Dogma 207, 222

Don't Look Now 57, 178

Dr. Strangelove or: How I Learned to Stop Worrying and Love the Bomb 44, *45*

Dunkirk 65

The Dust Bowl 205, *205*

E

Early Man 183, *183*

Easy Rider 84, *84*

Edward Scissorhands 136

The Emperor's New Groove 179

Escape from New York 228

Escape From Tomorrow 40

Executive Decision 160

The Exorcist 175, 200, *201*

Eyes Wide Shut 120

F

Fahrenheit 451 88, 89

Fantastic Mr Fox 134

Fear and Loathing in Las Vegas 88, 89

Fight Club 177

Firefox 28

The Florida Project 40

Forrest Gump 9, 26, 104

47 Meters Down 109

The 40 Year-Old Virgin 83

4.3.2.1 140

Four Weddings and a Funeral 41, *41*

Frankenstein 135, 136, 224

Frankenweenie 18

Frankie and Johnny 97

Friday 49

The Fugitive 44, 45

Full Metal Jacket 64

G

Gandhi 41

Geostorm 193, 215

Gigantic 33

The Godfather 46, 47, *47*, 129, 182

Godzilla 50, 228

Gone With the Wind 162

Goodfellas 106, 146, 199

The Goonies 171, *171*

The Grand Budapest Hotel 134, *134*

Gravity 80, *81*

Grease 186, *186*

The Greatest Show on Earth 176

The Greatest Showman 120

Gremlins 14, 18, 44

H

Halloween 77, 117

The Hangover 122

Hard Boiled 144, *144*

Harold and Maude 61

Harry Potter 18, 168

Hell's Angels 100, *101*

The Hidden Fortress 141, *141*

High Noon 30, 176, *176*

Howard 58

Hulk 15

The Hunger Games 109

I

I See a Dark Stranger 208

Ice Age 118

Ideal Home 23

Inception 11, *16*, 17

Independence Day 169

Indiana Jones 18, 44, 74, *74*, 160, 170

Inferno 171

Inglourious Basterds 52, *53*

Inside Out 66, *66*

Interstellar 24, *24*, 205, *205*

It Follows 15

It's a Mad, Mad, Mad, Mad World 202, *202*

It's a Wonderful Life 83

J

Jackass 148–9

Jackie Brown 199

James Bond (007) 70, *70*, 96, 172, 210, 225

Jaws   96, 109, 146, 193
Jurassic Park   36, 62

K

Kill Bill   62
King Kong   36, 37, *37*, 162
Kingdom of the Sun   179, *179*
The King's Speech   223

L

Labyrinth   69
The Lady Vanishes   208, *208*
Land of the Dead   211, *211*
Lee, Stan   54, 203, *203*
Les Misérables   168, *168*
Lethal Weapon   156, 198, 204
The Little Mermaid   58, 218
To Live and Die In L.A.   226
Logan   120

M

Mad Max   148, 175
Magnolia   126, 195
Mallrats   203, *203*
The Manchurian Candidate   46
Mars Attacks!   169
Marwencol   132
The Mask   153
The Matrix   158, 215, 227
Maverick   204
Mimic   147
Misery   217, *217*
Mission: Impossible   9, 39, 52,
    53, 120, 144, 150–1, 180

*Monty Python's Life of
    Brian*   163, *163*
mother!   136, 137
The Mummy   196
The Muppets   184, *184*, 215

N

The Naked Gun   76, *76*, 167
In the Name of the Father   220
Natural Born Killers   127
Night of the Living Dead   124,
    124
*The Night They Raided
    Minsky's*   175
Night Train to Munich   208,
    208
*A Nightmare on Elm
    Street*   212
1984   155
North by Northwest   49, *49*

O

Oliver!   170
*Once Upon a Time in
    America*   26
*Once Upon a Time in the
    West*   30
*One Flew Over the Cuckoo's
    Nest*   64, *64*
Our Daily Bread   139
Out of Sight   178, 199

P

Parfumerie   72
The Passion of the Christ   52

Patriot Games   52
Paul   211
Pet Sematary   200, 201, *201*
Pillow Talk   23, *23*
Pocahontas   179, 218
Porky's   109
Predator   197, 198
Pride   87, 96
Project A Part II   148, 149
Psycho   13

R

Ralph Breaks the Internet   154
Ready Player One   96, 131,
    132, 164
Red Heat   119
*The Revenge of
    Frankenstein*   135
Rififi   150
*Rita Hayworth and Shawshank
    Redemption* (book)   181
Robin Hood   221
RoboCop   136, 140
Rocky   79, *79*, 215
*The Rocky Horror Picture
    Show*   135
Royal Wedding   92, *92*

S

Safety Last!   85, *85*
The Santa Claus   177
Saving Mr. Banks   40
Saving Private Ryan   96, 192, *192*
Schindler's List   60
School of Rock   43

Scott Pilgrim vs. the World   18, 138

Searching   9

Shallow Grave   230

The Shape of Water   131, 147

The Shawshank Redemption   181

The Shining   131, 170, 191

The Shop Around the Corner   72

The Silence of the Lambs   22, 206, *206*

Singin' in the Rain   231

Sisters   145, *145*

Sixteen Candles   207

The Sixth Sense   161

Snake Eyes   145

The Social Network   50

Some Like It Hot   60

The Sound of Music   98, *98*

Spider-Man   153, 196

Splash   131

Star Trek   97

Star Wars   11, 36, 141, *141*, 157, *157*, 160, 163, 187, 190

Steamboat Bill, Jr.   148, 149, *149*

Stewart, James   146

Stuart Little   161, *161*

Sunset Boulevard   95, 197

Superman   88, 136, 167, 180

Supernova   182

Swordfish   125

Syriana   52, 53

T

Tag   187

Taxi Driver   62, *63*, 95

The Terminator   36, 75, 111

The Thing   55

This Is Spinal Tap   138

Titanic   190

Tootsie   87, *87*

Top Secret!   167

Total Recall   24

Toy Story   37, 48

Trading Places   125

The Transporter   202

TRON   36

Tropic Thunder   195

True Romance   121

The Truman Show   166, *166*

12 Angry Men   229, *229*

20th Century Fox   188

21 Jump Street   34

24   176

Twister   143

Two Mules for Sister Sara   104, 105, *105*

2001: A Space Odyssey   150, 185, *185*

U

The Untouchables   21, *21*

The Usual Suspects   26

V

Venom   196

Vertigo   146, *146*

A Very Brady Sequel   18

W

West Side Story   156

Westworld   36

When Harry Met Sally...   23, 72

When the Shooting Stops, the Cutting Begins   175

Who Framed Roger Rabbit   198

Willy Wonka & the Chocolate Factory   220, *220*

Windtalkers   144

The Wizard of Oz   9, 11, 143

Wonder   200, *200*

Wreck-It Ralph   18

The Wrong Man   212, *213*

Wyatt Earp   31

X

X-Men   120

Y

Yes Man   200

Young Sherlock Holmes   36, 37, *37*

You've Got Mail   72

Z

Zodiac   50

Zootopia   33

ACKNOWLEDGEMENTS

There's an inherent unfairness in books. That one person gets their name on the cover, yet the actual effort of getting this collection of words and pictures to you involves a Herculean effort by a whole bunch of wonderful people. Please indulge me while I say nice things about them.

I've got to start with the mighty overlord, Trevor Davies. A man who may have questionable skills when it comes to a pub quiz, yet when you want a human being to believe in you, to push you, to support you and back you, he's your man. Heck, he even buys you a coffee. Trevor: in the midst of a year and a half that we could both comfortably describe as testing, you've been an absolute bright light. Thank you.

But then so has Pollyanna The Poulter. Had she not become the person who made books happen, and happen on time, there are many other vocations that stand out. Polly could, for instance, be hired out to nations to get their trains running on time, or she could negotiate treaties to a schedule between differing governments. Thank the lord she landed here, though. And she even found time to get married in the middle of it all!

Super-duper Sonya Newland, from her luxurious-ish dwelling in Bristol, held words to account, asked questions, made things better, and drank tea. As always, she was and is invaluable, and continues to make my work look a lot better than it otherwise would be.

Talking of which, so do the crack commando design team on this tome. When we originally nattered about what we wanted this book to be, we knew we were setting a layout challenge. And that's when the powers of the universe brought us Jack Storey and James Round. I am eternally grateful they did. The universe wasn't done, though, because then in came the picture research ninjas, Giulia Hetherington, Jennifer Veall and Nick Wheldon, and production controller Grace O'Byrne. These people are all 23 per cent cleverer and more efficient than I could ever dream to be.

I'm not done yet. On the words front, I had help and support from Ryan Lambie, Louisa Mellor and Dan "Daniel" Cooper, and I thank them for letting me include the fruits of their brains too.

To Lindsey Williams for her fact-checking and for being Lindsey.

To Hedda, who has the end-of-level-boss job of being my agent: yikes! We did it! Thank you for being you. I like that you're on my side!

To Mark Kermode, Emma Turner, Elizabeth Donoghue, Chris Green and David King: huge thanks for your support.

To Deb: thank you. Hope she'd have liked this one.

To Irene: it might just have been worth the sunburn!

To my brilliant dad: well, heck. Thank you. Too much to say, too little space. Told you it was worth watching all those films, though (even though most of these aren't sold at the garden centre).

To my late, great mum: forever thank you. Miss you always.

To my favourite trilogy of all time: Eliot, Isabel and Thomas. This one's for you, kids. Thanks for putting up with a grumpy old nerd like me!

And finally, to all of the people who have supported my work, and continue to do so, my heartfelt thanks. I'll try not to let you all down.